thetasteofsummer

thetasteofsummer

INSPIRED RECIPES FOR CASUAL ENTERTAINING

by DIANE ROSSEN WORTHINGTON
COMPLETELY REVISED AND IN COLOR

with wine notes by Anthony Dias Blue
Photographs by Maura McEvoy

CHRONICLE BOOKS
SAN FRANCISCO

To my parents, Ruth and Allan Rossen, who gave me the gift of so many wonderful summers

acknowledgments

ETHAN ELLENBERG, FOR MAKING THIS HAPPEN; BILL LEBLOND, FOR HIS BELIEF IN THE BOOK AND THOUGHTFUL IDEAS; ANTHONY DIAS BLUE, FOR HIS UNIQUE KNOWLEDGE ON PAIRING WINE AND FOOD; CATHI RIMALOWER, FOR HER COMPUTER EXPERTISE; MICHAEL AND LAURA, FOR ALWAYS BEING THERE.

Library of Congress Cataloging-in-Publication
Data available.

ISBN 0-8118-2468-3

Printed in Hong Kong.

Prop styling by Christina Wressell
Food styling by Roscoe Betsill
Designed by Deborah Bowman
Typesetting by Deborah Bowman

The photographer wishes to thank the stores: *Home Goods* and *Kicking Stones* of Margaretville, New York, and *Brooke's Variety* and *Mercantile* of Andes, New York . . . And Marlene Niehaus for pulling it all together.

Distributed in Canada by Raincoast Books
8680 Cambie Street
Vancouver, British Columbia V6P 6M9

10 9 8 7 6 5 4 3 2 1

Chronicle Books
85 Second Street
San Francisco, CA 94105

www.chroniclebooks.com

Table of Contents

introduction

author's note

In this revised collection of my favorite recipes for summertime cooking and entertaining, I've kept some signature dishes from the first volume and have updated others with fresh ideas designed to make them even more appealing for the way we cook today. I've also created some wonderful recipes just for this edition.

Summer, with its balmy days, starry nights, bright flowers, and luscious fruits and vegetables, is reason enough to celebrate. This is a season for indulgence and spontaneity, a time for casual get-togethers. When it comes to summer entertaining, it's the food itself, with its vibrant colors and intense flavors, that becomes the focus. Precious free moments are meant for enjoying the outdoors, not polishing silver, arranging place cards, or toiling countless hours in the kitchen. It's much more fun to plan picnics, barbecues, and simple buffets—meals that can either be prepared quickly or require minimal last-minute attention. This informal style gives the host or hostess maximum time with family and friends, yet still allows for serving exciting and elegant food.

The culinary treasures summer offers are, of course, the best of the year. Perfect peak-of-flavor produce, the cornerstone of summer cooking, is available everywhere. It's easy to create wonderful dishes with the inspiration of this extraordinary bounty. Any summer meal is automatically enhanced by fresh-picked corn so sweet you'll want to eat it raw and tomatoes so red you'd swear they've been painted. And how can anyone resist a golden apricot, with its delicate balance between sweet and tart?

Fresh herbs also star in summer cooking. Fortunately, herbs are accommodating, growing as happily in tiny pots on apartment windowsills as they do in country gardens. One of my greatest everyday pleasures is stepping outside to snip fragrant basil leaves for pesto. Although herbs are available year-round, the intensity and distinctive flavor they develop in the hot months give a kind of magic to a dish, plus they can contribute beyond their role as seasonings stirred into a dish.

Potted herbs can serve as fragrant, appealing decorations simply by being whisked from the windowsill to the dinner table. Their flowers, especially those of basil, thyme, chives, and society garlic, make tasty garnishes, as well as delivering charming notes of color to contrast or highlight the foods of the season. Lavender chive blossoms, for example, can be sprinkled over yellow-squash soup or a yellow-and-green vegetable frittata—gorgeous.

Flowers are one of the easiest and most accessible garnishes, transforming the simplest dish into a still life of summer. Used in impromptu arrangements as table accents, they always look fresh and lovely. Pretty bouquets are easy to create. A drift of wildflowers freshly picked from a meadow, or a bunch of daisies purchased from a supermarket, can look just as beautiful and more in keeping with the season than a sophisticated centerpiece.

Of course, the most important showcase of summer entertaining, the constant backdrop, is the pleasant weather. Gentle breezes, blue skies, and warm temperatures are guaranteed to spark a spontaneous gaiety among guests. Eating outdoors, whether on the terrace of a city apartment, a deck overlooking the beach, or a spacious lawn, is always a pleasure. It creates a school's-out atmosphere that seems to bring on high spirits.

In summer, great style can be achieved with a minimum of effort. Spreading a quilt on a patch of grass for a casual candlelight dinner for two can be as appealing as an elegant patio buffet. Even table settings take on less significance. There's no need to fuss over matching place mats and napkins. Contrasting colors and patterns simply bring the table alive. At this time of year, anything goes, and if there is one rule, it's Less Is More. Attractive, sturdy paper plates set inside wicker holders can make an outdoor table look as festive as one set with gold-rimmed porcelain and crystal goblets. In summer, it's easy to be imaginative with what you have on hand—baskets, crocks, preserving jars—so look at your house with a fresh eye to the many possibilities.

The relaxed mood of the season should set the tone on special occasions, too. Graduation and wedding parties often call for fine china and cut glass, but these traditional celebrations can take on a more casual character in summer. Fresh flowers, fresh produce, and mild weather combine to create a lighthearted atmosphere. You can prepare dishes that are easy to make, like Chicken Salad Niçoise, Assorted Grilled Vegetable Platter, Whole Poached Salmon with Pesto-Cucumber Sauce, and Green Bean, Yellow Pepper, Jicama, and Tomato Salad, and serve them with nonchalant elegance.

The foods of summer should never require long hours of preparation. In fact, a number of dishes in this book are essentially uncooked. Grilling and sautéing replace more time-consuming cooking methods. Sauces are made quickly, whether they are a reduction of a marinade or a combination of a few harmonious ingredients. Making your own bread in the heat of the season is unappealing, so breads should either be quick and crisp or bought from the best bakery. Cooking that generates heat in the kitchen is kept to a minimum, with any necessary roasting or baking completed in the early morning.

Of course, sensational summer foods are comprised of more than just time-saving techniques. I like to base new recipes on classical ideas, yet combine some ingredients in unusual ways to create an element of surprise. For example, in the first-course chapter you'll find Guacamole Salsa. A combination of the best attributes of guacamole and salsa, this crunchy mixture of colorful vegetables and diced avocado is a perfect dip for tortilla chips or raw vegetables. A Thai-style satay is prepared with spicy pork tenderloin rather than chicken or beef. Instead of the traditional peanut sauce, it's accompanied by an orange-cilantro cream, adding an unexpected taste.

A particular advantage of summer entertaining is that there is no need to plan a traditional menu. On an exceptionally warm evening, three appetizers might make a complete meal. When a favorite vegetable, such as corn, is at its height of sweetness, you might put together an entire menu around it. One of my most successful dinner parties was a feast of Corn-Leek Cakes, Corn Chowder with Red Peppers, and Green Corn Tamales with Sour Cream–Tomatillo Sauce. Or you might opt for a communal feast and ask each guest to bring a dish based on a prized item from his or her garden or the local produce stand.

The recipes in the book are arranged by courses, and most of them are accompanied by menu and wine suggestions. Although entertaining is emphasized, you will discover that many of the dishes are equally appropriate for family meals. Most are quickly assembled or the work can be divided into stages and prepared partially in advance. Boxes sprinkled throughout offer informal recipes and useful information.

This book is designed to be flexible. You can follow the menu suggestions given for most recipes, or you can come up with your own menu tailored to a specific occasion. I have also included menus for such festive events as picnics, outdoor concerts, and buffets. You'll find these recipes are fun to prepare, and even those with many steps are easy to follow. Most of all, this food is designed to celebrate the splendid tastes of summer, while freeing you to enjoy the rest of its bountiful pleasures.

Cooking Over an Open Fire

Cooking in the summer will more often than not find you standing in front of a barbecue. While we all know how to throw a steak on the grill, there are some fine points to grilling that will make all the difference in the final result.

types of grills

There are three basic types of grill: the portable (the hibachi, for example) the open barbecue or brazier, and the covered barbecue. Portable ones are great for picnics and tailgate parties, but they don't have the flexibility to cook large amounts at one time or to cook thick pieces of meat without burning. Open models are best for quick-grilling foods that are no more than 1½ inches thick. Long, slow cooking cannot be achieved on an open fire, since there is no cover to trap the smoke and keep down the flame. Covered barbecues, which come in all shapes and sizes, provide the option of cooking the food covered or uncovered. There's usually an adjustable rack to allow more alternatives when cooking and timing any food. Certain foods, like butterflied leg of lamb and pizza (yes, pizza!), cook best covered.

There are some other factors to consider when shopping for a barbecue. Gas grills are a convenient alternative to regular charcoal grilling. While they may not satisfy the purist, they have become an acceptable option. These cookers are almost always equipped with a cover and usually have permanent "briquettes" made of rock. A gas-fueled flame heats the rock in lieu of the standard charcoal fire. The main disadvantage of these grills is that the food will not have the full smoky flavor most people expect. This drawback can be partially overcome by adding soaked, aromatic hardwood chips to the fire. The greatest benefits of gas grills are the quick heat-up time and the ability to cook food over even heat for long periods.

fuel for the fire

There's an ongoing debate over which fuel is best. Not so long ago only one choice existed, the charcoal briquette. But times have changed, and so has the fuel you can use to stoke up your barbecue. Hardwood charcoal is the new alternative.

Charcoal briquettes were initially invented by Henry Ford for industrial purposes. But he sold out to the Kingsford company, whose name became synonymous with barbecuing. The briquettes are made from wood scraps that have been burned into carbon. They are often mixed with fillers and additives, to keep them burning longer and faster. Some brands even give the food an off taste. If you use charcoal briquettes, let the coals reach an ashen-gray state, which indicates that the chemicals have burned off, before adding the food to the grill. Don't cook over charcoal that has even the smallest amount of black remaining.

Hardwood charcoals are more expensive but contain no chemicals. They are chunks of wood that have been carbonized, and the more common varieties include oak, maple, cherry, hickory, alderwood, and mesquite. Mesquite is the most popular hardwood today because it is plentiful and relatively inexpensive. The idea that mesquite charcoal will overwhelm the taste of the food is a popular misconception. It is true of mesquite wood, which produces much more smoke and thus a more intense flavor. But the charcoal adds only a light smoky-sweet flavor. I particularly like to use it when grilling chicken and meat.

Wood chips, including alder, hickory, cherry, apple, and oak, are another source of fuel. They are often used in addition to other fuel to add flavor: Soak the chips in water for a half hour before tossing them over the coals. You can also place them in a small aluminum pan on top of the lava briquettes in a gas grill to impart a smoky flavor to gas-grilled food.

Branches of fresh herbs—rosemary, fennel, bay, tarragon—thrown into the fire will contribute a subtle aroma and flavor to the food. Soak the branches first to make them smoke slowly. Grapevine cuttings may also be used.

how to start the fire

There are several ways to get your barbecue going. I grew up on charcoal fires ignited with lighter fluid. While this gets the fire blazing, the aftertaste the fuel passes along to the grilled food makes it a less than desirable choice. A trickier method is to use hot air. My husband's favorite technique is to light crumpled newspaper placed under the briquettes. He then uses a hair dryer on high to blow air onto the coals. Believe it or not, it really works. That would not be my first choice for a dinner party, however. The chimney starter, available in gourmet cookware and barbecue stores, is an easier and healthier way to ignite briquettes. The briquettes go in the top of the cylinder and crumpled newspaper goes in the bottom. You then place the chimney in the barbecue and light the newspaper. No lighter fluid is needed. The charcoal will ignite in about fifteen minutes. Other methods include using an electric starter or kindling. Whichever technique you choose, try to avoid using lighter fluid.

when is the fire ready?

Knowing just when to put your food on the fire is crucial to successful grilling. A fire that is too hot will char the outside of the food, while leaving the center raw. If it is too cool, the food won't cook properly.

Charcoal and wood fires are ready thirty to forty-five minutes after lighting. For most foods, the coals should have a layer of gray ash. If the flame is still high, the fire is not quite ready.

Medium-high-heat grilling: The fire should have red-hot coals with just a thin layer of gray ash and an occasional flare-up. Test the heat by holding your hand about six inches from the grid. You should be able to keep it there for only a few seconds. Medium-high-heat grilling is excellent for boneless chicken breasts or thin pieces of seafood, poultry, or meat.

Medium-heat grilling: The coals should be covered with a thick layer of gray ash and there should be no flames. This is a good fire for cooking thicker pieces of meat or poultry. You may want to cover your grill for this lower-temperature cooking.

grilling times and temperatures

These basic guidelines will tell you how long and at what temperature to cook, but remember that the food will continue cooking off the grill because it retains heat. Plan on removing it a few minutes before it is perfectly done.

FISH

Fish steaks and fillets are best cooked on an open grill over medium-high heat. Brush the fish liberally with oil before placing it on the grill to prevent sticking. If you're grilling a whole fish, a hinged basket allows you to turn the fish easily. Cook whole fish over medium heat using a cover. Cooking times will vary with the type of fish and its thickness. Check it with a fork; it should just begin to flake. Avoid overcooking fish, as both the texture and the taste will change.

POULTRY

Cook most poultry on a covered grill over medium heat. It requires longer and slower cooking than fish or red meat. Boned chicken breasts and turkey slices are the exception; they cook quickly over medium-high heat. Boneless chicken breasts require 6 to 8 minutes on each side, while chicken pieces require 8 to 14 minutes on each side. Use these times as guidelines for other types of poultry.

If you don't have a covered grill, baste poultry often to retain moisture and allow a slightly longer cooking time. Wait until a thick layer of gray ash covers the coals before you begin cooking, to ensure an even temperature.

MEATS

An instant-read thermometer is handy for testing any large piece of meat for doneness. You may want to take the meat off the heat 5° before it reaches the desired temperature, since it will rise an additional 5° once it is removed. General temperature guidelines follow.

Beef and lamb should register 130°F to 135°F for rare, 135°F to 145°F for medium-rare, and 150°F for medium. Pork roasts should reach 160°F. Do not let them rise above that, or the meat will be dry. Steaks and chops are cooked according to the thickness of the cut. Sear them on each side for 30 seconds, and then cook according to the following times, with the lower number indicating the time for rare and the higher number for well done. The times for each side: 1 inch, 3 to 6 minutes; 1½ inches, 4 to 9 minutes; 2 inches, 6 to 10 minutes. Do not poke the meat with a fork to test for doneness. Juices will be released and the meat will dry out. Season the meat with salt and pepper after it is cooked.

VEGETABLES

Clean the vegetables and slice them if necessary for the grill. Blanch certain vegetables, such as pearl onions and summer squashes, in boiling water for one minute to eliminate the raw taste that quick grilling might leave. Brush the vegetables with extra-virgin olive oil or avocado oil before placing them on the grill. Sear them over medium-high heat to seal in their juices and then move them to the side of the grill to finish cooking. Thinly sliced vegetables will take six to ten minutes on each side. Vegetables that fall apart easily, such as sliced tomatoes or onions, should be placed in a grilling basket. All vegetables can be skewered on metal or bamboo skewers if desired, but remember to soak bamboo skewers for at least a half hour before grilling.

FRUITS

Thread sliced apples, bananas, pears, peaches, nectarines, or pineapples on skewers and grill over medium-high heat for just a few minutes on each side.

some handy tools

When barbecuing, it's helpful to have these utensils on hand:

- Basting brushes, especially wide ones with long handles, are necessary for basting. Or you can use branches of fresh herbs such as rosemary.
- An instant-read thermometer is good for checking when thick pieces of meat or roasts are done.
- A grilling basket with a long handle is indispensable for grilling whole fish and certain vegetables.
- A wicker basket is useful near the grill. Line it with a colorful napkin or tea towel and fill it with pot holders, a spray bottle of water for flare-ups, a flashlight, a long-handled fork, tongs, a large knife, and a spatula.

preparing and cleaning the grill

Although some grill cooks believe that subsequent fires will burn off the residue from the last cookout, excusing you from cleaning the grill, it's untrue. In fact, you have to clean the grid—the cooking surface—every time you use it, or the food will pick up off tastes. To make it easier, check the manufacturer's instructions for specific details.

Use a crumpled ball of aluminum foil to clean the grid while it is still lukewarm. Afterward, wipe it with a wet sponge or paper towels. Stiff barbecue brushes also come in handy, but check the manufacturer's instructions carefully because you can damage a chrome or porcelain grid. Occasionally, it is necessary to wash the entire grill with soapy water. As a preventive measure, I frequently brush the grid with a mild vegetable or olive oil to keep food from sticking and burning.

marinades

Marinades are assembled in moments and work wonders with grilled foods, both tenderizing and adding flavor. They are usually made with a combination of an acid, such as citrus juice, vinegar, wine, or even yogurt, and vegetable or olive oil. A good ratio is two parts acid to one part oil. Spices, herbs, and mustards are added for specific flavors. Always let the marinade rest for a few minutes before adding the food, to allow the flavors to develop. Use only glass, stainless steel, porcelain, or enamel vessels for marinating; aluminum imparts a metallic taste. Be sure all the surfaces of the food are covered with the marinade.

There are a few general rules to remember when marinating: Thick pieces of meat can be marinated for up to twenty-four hours without causing a change in texture. Generally, poultry needs less time, up to six hours. Fish should never be marinated for more than two hours if the acid content of the marinade is high, because the marinade will actually cook the fish.

A FEW OTHER TIPS:

- If you are marinating food in the refrigerator, remove it a half hour before grilling to let it reach room temperature.
- Don't forget to marinate vegetables, as they are excellent when flavored before grilling.
- Pastes or herb coatings are other types of marinades, although they are used more to flavor than to tenderize.

Picnics

Picnics are certainly the most relaxed style of summer entertaining. The preparation can be as impromptu as stopping by the local deli and picking up what looks good, or as time-consuming as making pâtés, salads, entrées, sauces, and desserts for days. I enjoy both. My most memorable picnic was spent with a cooking school group high in the French Alps on a warm summer day. We had prepared food for the picnic in class the night before and then bought fresh tomatoes and peaches at the local market. While the meal was superb, what made it unforgettable was the breathtaking mountaintop setting, the bright sunlight streaming down, and the warmth of the moment. It's good to remember that the food is only part of a picnic's appeal. The setting, the company, and the time of day each adds its distinct contribution.

My favorite picnics tend to be midafternoon lunches, wine and hors d'oeuvres at sunset, and outdoor concert dinners. While picnics may take place in a variety of settings—in a meadow blanketed with brilliant flowers, by a cold mountain stream, in a city park, on a sandy beach, on a sailboat—the secrets of all successful picnics are essentially the same.

Probably the single most important item to ensure a perfect picnic is a good food chest or cooler. Many different types are available today, so you can choose one that will fill your particular needs. If you only go on picnics for two, a large cooler is probably unnecessary and cumbersome. If you usually picnic with a large group, you may want to invest in a couple of sizes that will easily accommodate assorted shapes. It's also helpful to be able to separate the cold dishes from the warm ones. Different-sized packets of "blue ice," those rectangles of frozen blue gel that keep food chilled, stored in your freezer will allow you to picnic on a moment's notice. Solidly frozen blue ice will usually keep already chilled food very cold for three or four hours.

A number of coolers for wine are marketed as well. Some hold two bottles and several glasses. I like to carry a double cooler filled with wine and sparkling water.

Make a menu ahead of time and tape it to your refrigerator. Check off each dish as you pack it into your basket. There's nothing worse than arriving with everything except that one important sauce or salad dressing.

Depending on your mood and the menu, you can take as little paraphernalia or as much as you like. The following is a detailed list to help make your picnic easy and carefree.

- A picnic basket, hamper, or tote bag for carrying food and equipment
- Food chests to keep food hot or cold
- Frozen blue ice for chilled foods
- A tablecloth, quilt, sheet, or other ground cover
- Large cloth or paper napkins
- Wicker holders for paper plates
- Plates for appetizer, soup, main course, and dessert
- Coffee cups, waterglasses, and wineglasses
- Flatware and serving pieces
- Bottle opener, corkscrew, and can opener
- Paper towels
- Plastic bags or plastic wrap for leftovers
- Large plastic bag for trash
- Large plastic bag for soiled dishes and utensils
- Small cutting board and knife
- Salt, pepper, sugar, cream for coffee, mustard, relish, and other condiments
- Fuel and matches if using a hibachi
- Ice, liquor, and mixes
- Thermos filled with hot coffee
- Soft drinks, water, sparkling water, beer, and/or wine
- Whole lemons and limes
- Candles, candle holders, and matches
- Flashlight

Packing and serving food on a picnic requires careful planning. These tips will help to ensure your food arrives as fresh as when it left the kitchen.

- Pack the foods to be eaten last at the bottom of the bag or chest and those to be eaten first on top, so that you don't have to unpack everything at once.
- Use vacuum-packed containers to avoid leaks and soggy bags, taping the lids with masking tape for extra reinforcement. Seal the containers in lock-top plastic bags.
- Pack soft foods like deviled eggs, tomatoes, or fruit in hard plastic containers or egg cartons.
- If you are serving a hot soup, preheat the thermos with boiling water. For a cold soup, chill the thermos with ice water for several minutes.
- Divide or cut the portions in your kitchen. It's much easier to serve pieces or slices of grilled chicken or duck than to carve them on site.
- Pack garnishes in lock-top plastic bags, sprinkling parsley, basil, mint, and herb flowers with water before packing. Keep them in a cooler.

Finally, strictly observe these practices to avoid food spoilage:

- Mayonnaise keeps well in a jar but spoils quickly when added to a salad or sandwich. As a precaution, keep the mayonnaise chilled in the cooler, and dress salads or sandwiches at the picnic site rather than at home.
- Keep eggs, dairy products, and uncooked meats well chilled until just before cooking and/or serving.
- Make sure there is sufficient breathing room in the cooler to keep the cold air circulating. Don't jam it full, or the temperature will rise.
- Don't partially cook the food at home and finish it at the picnic site, as the food will be at the optimum temperature for bacterial invasion during transportation.
- Pack the food just before leaving for the picnic.

the no-cook picnic

This extremely easy menu takes a little forethought, since the gravlax requires three to four days to cure in the refrigerator.

Chilled Avocado Soup with Tomato-Cucumber Salsa

Basil Gravlax with Sweet Mustard-Basil Sauce

Assorted Pumpernickel and Whole-Wheat Rolls

Chilled Red and White Radishes, Carrots, and Cucumbers

A Wicker Tray of Fresh Goat Cheese, Mascarpone, Gorgonzola, and Sharp Cheddar

A Basket of Nectarines, Plums, and Apricots

Assorted Cookies

a barbecue picnic

This high-spirited picnic is based on the exhilarating flavors of Latin food. It's easy to assemble once you solve the problem of transporting the grill. A small hibachi will work fine. The beans, marinade, and fruit can be made a day ahead. Wrap the pot of hot beans in a tablecloth or in a few sheets of crumpled newspaper to keep it warm. The Guacamole Salsa and Papaya Salsa are best made the same day. Thread the shrimp onto bamboo skewers that will fit in a plastic container and marinate them in the same container. If you have time, bake the cookies just a few hours before serving or choose your favorite packaged cookies. Mexican beer is great with this menu.

Guacamole Salsa

Tortilla Chips

Tequila-Lime Grilled Shrimp

Cuban Black Beans

Tomato-Papaya-Mint Salsa

Slices of Yellow and Red Seedless Watermelon

Toasted Almond Cookies with Lemon and Port

an outdoor concert picnic

This sensational picnic menu can be served as simply or as elegantly as you like. The soup can be made a day ahead and, depending on the weather, served hot or chilled. The chicken tastes best served warm, so roast it right before leaving and pack the sauce separately. Place the chicken in a heavy-duty plastic container and wrap the package in a tablecloth or several thicknesses of newspaper. The salad and asparagus can be assembled early in the morning. The tart may also be prepared at the same time or the night before.

Minted Chinese Snow Pea Soup

Crispy Roasted Chicken with Spinach Pesto Cream

Cracked Wheat–Vegetable Salad

Chilled Asparagus with Red Pepper Vinaigrette

Hazelnut-Plum Tart with Crème Fraîche

an elegant picnic

This is a favorite picnic menu when I'm in the mood for something luxurious. The soup, the green bean salad, and the poached peaches can be made early in the day. Keep the eggs, lobster, and dressing very cold. Assemble the lobster salad right before serving. Start with the soup in chilled mugs and then serve the eggs and two salads together.

Golden Summer Soup

Smoked Salmon Deviled Eggs

Cold Lobster Salad with Caviar-Dill Mayonnaise

Green Bean Salad with Yellow Pepper, Jicama, and Tomato

French Rolls

Poached Peaches in White Zinfandel with Raspberry Sauce

Toasted Almond Cookies with Lemon and Port

sunset picnic

Prepare the sauces and the eggplant the day before and assemble the dishes at the picnic. Baskets and serving trays decorated with herbs and herb blossoms will make this simple picnic fare special. To make a meal of it, add cold, sliced roast beef and sliced tomatoes.

Cold Shrimp with Ancho Chile Mayonnaise

Assorted Grilled Vegetable Platter

Roasted Eggplant with Balsamic Vinegar

Thinly Sliced French Bread

Champagne

Buffets

The buffet is a casual, easy style of entertaining that seems especially well suited to summer, when the spirit of easy living is most widely felt. Guests enjoy the unstructured atmosphere that a buffet offers. Even if the event is relatively formal, like a wedding, a buffet will loosen things up. It's certainly the easiest style for the host or hostess, since only minimal last-minute preparation is necessary if the day is well planned. Depending on the budget and your intentions, you can hire bartenders and kitchen help, rent everything from glasses to the tablecloth, and host a nearly professional party. Or you can create an extremely simple buffet that is produced by only one pair of hands in the kitchen. Probably the most important element in planning any party is being able to think through the entire event in detail, so that you avoid any pitfalls and leave yourself as free as possible to enjoy your guests.

the food

You can host a *grande bouffe*—an elaborate smorgasbord of dishes—or build the menu around a central dish supported by complementary dishes that won't overwhelm it. Choose foods that will not suffer if eaten warm rather than hot, or slightly chilled rather than cold. If you're not planning to have your guests sit down at tables, don't serve foods that need to be cut with a knife. Instead, choose precut bite-size food or food that can be picked up with fingers. Remember, your guests will already have a full plate of food, a napkin, and a wineglass to juggle.

Obviously, the more dishes you can completely prepare ahead of time, the better. Even if the main course is barbecued, consider grilling it a couple of hours in advance and serving it at room temperature. If a dish won't reheat successfully, forget it and choose something that will or that doesn't require any heating.

Make up a prep sheet for the meal, including all the shopping information, which day you will prepare the dish, and what it will be served on. Check off everything as you go. Be sure to consider serving amounts when planning your menu. You need to know exactly how many times to multiply each recipe.

You'll probably need extra cooling space. If you can't use a neighbor's refrigerator, set up a cooler or ice chest and use it for foods that only need to be chilled. Early in the day, rinse, dry, and tightly roll greens in tea towels so they'll take up minimal space in the crisper.

where to serve

Once you decide how many people to invite, you'll know what size space will accommodate them. If you are going to serve outside, my preference during the summer months, examine the space and decide where the buffet table should be placed. Keep in mind that the closer to the kitchen the table is, the easier it is to manage. Refilling platters, for instance, is much more convenient when the refrigerator is nearby. One suggestion is to serve in the dining room or the living room, even though people will then take their plates outside. This strategy will also avoid the problems of hovering insects and unreliable weather.

If you choose to serve on an outside buffet table, you can either arrange the buffet table against the wall, in the center of the patio or deck, or, for an especially large party, you can set up two tables to avoid long lines. You may want to place a separate dessert table in a different location so that guests who are finished with their entrées can move to another area. The dessert table should be near an electrical outlet so that you can serve coffee and tea on it, too.

the bar

Designate a separate area away from the main buffet table to set up your bar. A bartender is an enormous asset for a large party, but not essential. Arrange the mixers, liquors, red wine, glasses, garnishes, and napkins on a table or other convenient surface. An all-purpose wine goblet is a good choice for most drinks. You'll need a large ice bucket with a refill source under the table in a cooler. I like to have a large pitcher or punch bowl of a mixed drink like Bloody Marys or Sangria available. There should also be a large ice-filled washtub or cooler with a variety of soft drinks, white wine, or Champagne for the guests to help themselves. Put out an appetizer or two on the bar as well. For more specifics on how to set up a bar, refer to the Summer Drinks section.

the buffet table

There is no "right" way for the table to look. It is a matter of personal taste. Mixing and matching old and new, complementary—not matching—napkins and tablecloths, dishes, and serving pieces will create a warm and informal atmosphere.

tablecloths and napkins

If you would like to have a specific color scheme, start with the tablecloth and then match the napkins to it. Through the years I have collected an assortment of napkins in different colors and patterns that go with several solid-colored tablecloths. If you are serving barbecued dishes, nicely designed paper napkins may be best. Whatever table cover you choose, it should just barely touch the floor. Tables look pretty with a double covering. First, cover the table with a plain-colored tablecloth. Then fit either a square or a circular patterned cloth or lace tablecloth on top. If you don't want to purchase or create your own tablecloths, remember your local party-rental service.

plates and flatware

Matching plates are no more necessary than matching table linens. Alternate the dishes to create an interesting color pattern. If you want to invest in a set of buffet plates, I recommend large, plain white plates or clear glass ones because they adapt to any occasion and are inexpensive. Paper plates are sometimes appropriate for a very casual buffet. Choose a sturdy, attractive plate that can handle a full meal. Fitting paper plates into inexpensive wicker holders stabilizes them. Stack the plates at the beginning of the buffet line next to the flatware.

My favorite way to present the cutlery is to wrap it in a napkin, tie a bow around it with either ribbon or jute, and then tuck a fresh herb blossom or flower into the bow. If that sounds too elaborate, skip the ties and arrange the napkin rolls in a basket. You can either pile them on top of one another or stand them up with the handles on the bottom. Or just lay them neatly on the table.

glasses

Mix and match whatever glasses you have on hand. For a large party, consider renting all-purpose wineglasses. Figure on doubling the number of guests to arrive at the correct number of glasses. For a more informal party, use thick plastic glasses. If you're serving Champagne, use Champagne flutes. You can buy them, rent them, or use plastic ones, but the shape is essential.

serving pieces

Serving bowls and platters in a variety of different styles and materials will bring an added dimension to the table. You can mix pewter, glass, wood, china, and pottery in an array of shapes: round, rectangular, square, even sculptured. For added interest, try altering the height of some of the dishes by placing the bowls or platters on pedestals.

centerpieces

The main centerpiece is the food, especially when it is attractively displayed and garnished with colorful edible flowers and herb blossoms. Think of it as a still life. A basket of simply arranged flowers is always welcome, but make sure it is not too tall. You may want to have small vases of flowering herbs placed next to a dish that features the same herb. To decide where to place the flowers, first set up the table with all the necessary serving pieces, so you won't have any last-minute surprises. Imagine what the colors of the various dishes will be and what type of arrangement would best complement them. Baskets of bright vegetables, such as red and yellow peppers, orange and red tomatoes, and different shapes of green and yellow squashes make a striking presentation. Shallow bowls of freshly picked flowers floating in water along with floating candles are also attractive. Or consider scattering assorted shapes and sizes of seashells in the center of the table and interspersing them with flowers for an unusual arrangement.

☼ making an ice ring

When serving punch, make an ice ring to create a spectacular presentation that will also keep the punch cool. Fill the ring with a colorful pattern of sliced fruits and mint leaves, freeze it, and place it in the punch bowl just before serving. The secret to making a beautiful ice ring is to use distilled water for clarity and to freeze the ring in successive layers, trapping the fruit and leaves together in the middle layer so they won't escape into the punch as the ring melts.

Fill a ring mold with distilled water to a depth of 2 inches and freeze. When frozen, place fruit or leaves on top and add water to a depth of ½ inch. Return the mold to the freezer until completely frozen. Fill the rest of the ring with distilled water and freeze completely. When you're ready to unmold it, dip the ring into a bowl of hot water for 15 seconds or rub the outside with a hot towel, then invert.

This is the season when beverages attract nearly as much attention as food. Hot days require the contrast of the coolest and most refreshing drinks possible. In order to prepare a variety of interesting and classic drinks at a moment's notice, have the necessary ingredients and assorted utensils within easy reach.

the summer bar

A summer bar can be as simple or as elaborate as the occasion demands. Frosty drinks made with vodka, tequila, gin, or rum and tonic or sparkling water are always popular in the hot months. Chilled wine, sangria, Campari, wine coolers, and beer are also welcome in the summer heat. Keep plenty of fresh juices and fruit nectars on hand to serve with sparkling water for a refreshing nonalcoholic beverage. Icy herbal teas and thirst-quenching mineral water are crowd pleasers, too.

A FULL BAR INCLUDES:

Vodka, gin, scotch, bourbon, whiskey, brandy, tequila, sweet and dry vermouth, Campari, various liqueurs (especially orange-flavored ones and amaretto), beer, and a selection of chilled white and red wines. Juices, soft drinks, tonic, sparkling water, bitters, grenadine, and sugar syrup will round out the supplies. Plan on about half a bottle of wine or two alcoholic beverages and soft drinks for each guest. One serving of liqueur for each guest should be adequate.

RECOMMENDED UTENSILS INCLUDE:

A jigger, measuring spoons, a citrus squeezer, a citrus stripper, a paring knife, a blender, an ice bucket, tongs, a cocktail shaker, a corkscrew, glasses in assorted sizes and shapes, and perhaps a pitcher or a punch bowl.

HAVE ON HAND GARNISHES SUCH AS:

Lemon, lime, and orange slices and mint sprigs. Sliced strawberries, peaches, nectarines, or kiwifruits also make attractive garnishes, adding a refreshing twist and a splash of color to your drinks.

some interesting drinks

Certain drinks never go out of style. Here are some old favorites, along with a few contemporary adaptations. Some of them call for the addition of sugar syrup, which is easily made by combining 1 cup sugar and 1 cup water over medium heat and stirring until the sugar is completely dissolved. This will keep refrigerated for up to 1 month.

pitcher or punch-bowl drinks

Andy's Pink Sangria:

Combine 4 parts White Zinfandel, 2 parts orange juice, 1 part lemon juice, 1 part Pimms Cup No. 1, and slices of lemons, oranges, limes, and peaches. Finish with sparkling water and a touch of sugar syrup, to taste. (You can also add frozen hulled strawberries as flavorful ice cubes. Freeze them on a baking sheet and drop them in right before serving.) For a party, plan on 1 bottle of Zinfandel for 4 people.

Margarita:

Combine 1½ ounces tequila, 1 ounce lime juice, 1 ounce Cointreau or Triple Sec, and cracked ice. Shake together in a cocktail shaker and serve, or whirl in a blender for a foamier drink. You can also add pureed strawberries, peaches, or even Crenshaw or honeydew melon. To serve, first dip the rim of a balloon glass in fresh lime juice, then swirl it in coarse salt. Serves 1, and may be multiplied as needed.

Strawberry Banana Daequiri:

In a blender, combine ½ cup rum with 1 cup strawberries, 1 sliced banana, the juice of ½ lemon, 1 to 2 tablespoons sugar syrup, and ice cubes to cover. Blend until frothy, pour into a pitcher or balloon glasses, and garnish with mint sprigs. Serves 2 and may be multiplied as needed.

individual drinks

Kir:

Pour ½ ounce crème de cassis into a wineglass and fill with chilled white wine.

Kir Royale:

Pour ½ ounce crème de cassis into a Champagne flute and fill with chilled dry Champagne.

Champagne Framboise:

Pour ½ ounce framboise liqueur into a Champagne flute and fill with chilled dry Champagne.

Bellini:

An inexpensive, slightly sweet, sparkling wine like Prosecco is recommended here. Use pureed unpeeled Babcock or other white peaches. Pour ¼ cup peach puree into a Champagne flute and top off with sparkling wine.

nonalcoholic beverages

Juices and nectars mixed with sparkling water are wonderful thirst quenchers on hot afternoons. Try these variations. For an added taste of fruit, make ice cubes out of fruit juice and use them in your coolers or tea. Or freeze pieces of fruit, such as chunks of peach, nectarine, or whole berries, and use them as clever and pretty additions to your drinks.

Tropical Cooler:

Mix 1 part guava nectar to 1 part fresh orange juice to 2 parts sparkling water. Float an orange slice on top.

Peach-Mint Sparkler:

Mix 1 part peach nectar to 4 parts sparkling water. Wedge a peach slice and a fresh mint sprig on the edge of the glass.

Pink Honeydew Spritzer:

Combine the puree of 1 medium pink honeydew with 2 tablespoons peeled and minced fresh ginger, 1 teaspoon lemon juice, 3 tablespoons chopped fresh mint, and 1 to 2 tablespoons sugar syrup. Add one-sixth of the mixture to each glass and fill with sparkling water. Garnish with fresh mint sprigs. Serves 6.

Citrus Mint Iced Tea:

Combine equal parts orange, lemon, and mint tea bags together with a cinnamon stick and fresh mint leaves in a heatproof bowl. Pour in boiling water and let stand for 30 minutes. Strain out the tea bags and mint leaves and pour the tea into a large pitcher that will fit in your refrigerator. Add water to reach your preferred strength and then chill until ice cold. You can add different fruit juices or nectars or fruit slices to the tea right before serving.

Iced Espresso:

Prepare espresso coffee in your regular coffee maker, doubling the usual amount of coffee. Place a spoon in each glass to keep it from cracking, pour the glass half full, and then fill it with ice.

a barbecue buffet

Serve the bruschetta with drinks while the barbecued brisket and ribs finish cooking. The coleslaw will taste even better if it's made the night before. Put the dessert on a separate table, with the biscuits stacked on a pretty plate, the strawberries in a glass bowl with a silver serving spoon, and the custard sauce in a bowl with a ladle, so that the guests can assemble their own shortcakes.

Bruschetta with Tomato, Basil, and Mozzarella

Barbecued Brisket of Beef and/or Sweet and Hot Spareribs
with Apricot-Plum Sauce

Colorful Coleslaw

Grilled Corn on the Cob with Ancho Chile Butter

Herbed Garlic Cheese Bread

Strawberry Shortcake with Raspberry Custard Sauce

a soup and salad buffet

All of these dishes can be prepared well in advance, keeping last-minute work to a minimum. Serve the soup in a tureen or pitchers for pouring into plastic or glass mugs. For a tempting dessert presentation, scoop out balls of vanilla ice cream a few hours before serving and place them on waxed paper to freeze. Right before serving, arrange them in a glass bowl next to the pie.

Minestrone with Pesto Cream

Chicken Salad with Roasted Garlic Mayonnaise

Green Bean Salad with Yellow Pepper, Jicama, and Tomato

Lattice Crust Pie with Rhubarb, Peaches, Strawberries, and Plums

French Vanilla Ice Cream

a sunday buffet brunch

Here's a hearty but easy menu to put together for a lazy Sunday afternoon.

Assorted Melon Slices

Summertime Frittata

Lemon-Herb Roasted Potatoes

Grilled Chicken, Veal, or Italian Sausages

Raspberry Pound Cake

Iced Coffee

a celebration buffet

Whether it's for a graduation, wedding, or birthday, this is a striking menu. Place the appetizers by the bar so that your guests can help themselves.

Crudité Baskets and Buttermilk Dressing with Garden Herbs and Roasted Red
  Pepper Mayonnaise

Goat Cheese and Pesto Torta with Hazelnuts

Thin Toasts

Grilled Chicken with Sun-Dried-Tomato Marinade

Gratin of Summer Squash with Leeks and Rice

Simple Green Salad with Summer Vinaigrette

Hot French and Sourdough Rolls

Chocolate Pecan Torte with Espresso Crème Anglaise

The Wines of Summer

BY ANTHONY DIAS BLUE

Back in the dark ages of wine writing—fifteen or twenty years ago—there was a lot of talk about rules. There were rules about which wine to serve with which food, rules about which glasses to use, rules about at what temperature wines should be served, and rules about which wines should be served first. All of this was a manifestation of the basic insecurity Americans felt about choosing the "right" wine. People needed strict guidelines to avoid the possibility of making a serious oenological faux pas.

Things are different today. Americans are more confident when it comes to wine and food. We have discovered the brilliance of our own modern cuisine and the consistent quality of our wines. We have a better understanding of foreign cuisines and imported wines. We are more assured about our own taste and much more relaxed about the choices that we must inevitably make.

There are no rules. The choice of wine no longer depends on a rigid set of commandments. Today, the selection depends more on our own tastes and sense of appropriateness than any strict doctrine.

If you hate Gewürztraminer, all the directives in the world dictating that variety will be useless. If you love sipping Chardonnay with steak, go ahead and drink it. In other words, pairing wine and food is a subjective exercise. Some people may like Sauvignon Blanc with salmon; others may prefer White Zinfandel or even Red Zinfandel with this rich fish. No choice is wrong.

Appropriateness, on the other hand, is an important consideration. Some years ago, my wife and I invited a group of friends, many of them avid wine lovers, to a beach party on a July weekend. We prepared pâtés, salads, grilled meats, and home-baked breads, but I wasn't sure which wine to serve. I finally settled on a great white Burgundy, an older Corton-Charlemagne.

The afternoon of the party was sunny and clear, our outdoor spread was resplendent, and the guests were in great spirits. They exclaimed over the lunch and the wine, but my heart fell when I saw one of my most knowledgeable friends frown as he took his first sip.

"What's wrong?" I asked him. "Isn't the wine good?"

"Of course it is," he responded. "The problem is that the wine is too good."

He was right. I had served a rich, complex, serious wine that completely overmatched the food. Light summer meals are meant to delight the palate with simple pleasures and not-so-serious tastes. The wines that accompany them should do the same.

Fresh, snappy, youthful wines are the answer. Grand wines are suited for grand cuisine on grand occasions. Bright and active summer days, and the kinds of dishes Diane Worthington has created, call for young, full-flavored, unintimidating wines.

Here are some very general pointers: Gewürztraminer does nicely when teamed with spicy foods. Try this assertive wine with seafood served in a peppery sauce or chicken with Mexican spices. Riesling and Chenin Blanc are wonderful picnic wines—lighthearted, fruity, and just a bit frivolous. Tangy, crisp Sauvignon Blanc has that steely quality that mates well with oysters or other seafood.

Chardonnay comes in a number of different styles. There are crisp versions, lush and fruity versions, and big, concentrated versions. This wide range makes Chardonnay a virtually all-purpose wine. The crisp style works well with seafood, pastas, salads, or light chicken dishes; the fruity style complements saucier, more highly seasoned dishes; and the heavy style should be matched with creamy sauces or with veal, pork, or even beef.

Zinfandel is a wonderful summer wine. It fills all the requirements: it's fresh, fruity, and at its best when young. Try a snappy, ruby-colored one with pasta, eggs, or meats, especially those served with spicy sauces.

Other reds—young Merlots, young Cabernet Sauvignons, spicy Beaujolais—are also appropriate for the season. Pour them with meats or pastas, and serve them slightly chilled. Rosé and "blush" wines are suitable warm-weather beverages, too. Have a tangy White Zinfandel with picnics, with pizza, with sandwiches.

Remember not to overlook the delightful crop of imports that fill the summer bill: Soave, Frascati, Orvieto, Bardolino, Valpolicella, Chianti, and Dolcetto wines from Italy; Mâcon, White Bordeaux, Vouvray, Beaujolais, and Alsatian wines from France; Chardonnay, Sauvignon, and Rhine Riesling from Australia; crisp whites from Germany, Spain, and Portugal.

The wines of summer are all around us. They are breezy and charming, and they make the foods of summer just that much more enjoyable.

keeping wine

Half-empty bottles of wine are often left over after entertaining. Don't just cork them and expect them to be drinkable the next day. The warm summer temperatures will oxidize your leftovers before you can say "vinegar barrel." After you have corked them, stick them in the refrigerator—yes, even the reds. When it's time to drink them, let them return to room temperature, which should take about a half hour.

There are a number of excellent, inexpensive devices on the market that pump nitrogen into the bottle and preserve the wine by protecting it from oxygen. Of course, the best way to make sure wine retains its freshness is to drink it up when it is first opened.

firstcourses
andappetizers

with tomato, basil, and mozzarella
bruschetta

SERVES 6–8

Enjoy this rustic Italian appetizer while the rest of your dinner is cooking on the grill. Prepare the topping a few hours ahead and when the coals are at their hottest put the bread on the grill.

 WITH MOZZARELLA AND GARLIC THE ANSWER HAS TO BE A YOUNG AND FRUITY CHIANTI OR ZINFANDEL, SERVED AT ROOM TEMPERATURE (60°F).

1. Dice the tomatoes into ½-inch pieces and drain over a bowl for 30 minutes to remove excess liquid.
2. Combine all topping ingredients except the cheese in a small nonreactive bowl. Stir well and taste for seasoning.
3. Prepare grill for medium-hot grilling. Place the bread on the grill and grill each side just until marks of the grill appear. Remove from grill and place on a serving platter. Rub the bread on each side with whole garlic cloves.
4. Add the cheese to the topping, spoon the mixture onto each bread slice, and then drizzle over a little more olive oil. Sprinkle with freshly ground pepper and serve.

Advance Preparation: The topping may be prepared up to 4 hours in advance through step 2 and refrigerated.

Topping
1 pound ripe plum (Roma) tomatoes, peeled and seeded

2 medium garlic cloves, minced

3 tablespoons finely chopped basil

1 tablespoon finely chopped Italian parsely

2 tablespoons extra virgin olive oil

salt and freshly ground black pepper

¼ pound fresh mozzarella cheese, cut into ½-inch dice

Bread
1 medium baguette, French, sourdough, or Italian bread, cut into ½-inch slices

2 large garlic cloves, peeled

2 tablespoons extra virgin olive oil

freshly ground black pepper

✳ preparing artichokes

1. With kitchen shears, cut off the sharp points from the leaves of each artichoke. Remove the small, dry outer leaves from around the base. Cut off the stem, leaving 1 inch intact.
2. Soak the artichokes in a sinkful of cold water for at least 15 minutes to clean them.
3. Place the artichokes upright in a pan. Pour in water to a depth of 4 inches and add some lemon slices and a drop of olive oil. Cover partially and cook over medium heat until the leaves easily pull free, 30 to 40 minutes. Remove from pan and let cool.
4. Serve cold with Summer Vinaigrette (page 182), Spinach Pesto Cream (page 57), or watercress, dill, and spinach mayonnaise (page 186).

guacamole salsa

Sometimes the whole is greater than the sum of its parts, as in this cross between a spicy vegetable salsa and a traditional guacamole. Beware: you'll love this crunchy dip. When I first prepared it, a few friends and I quickly consumed the whole bowl and wanted more. Crisp tortilla chips and some frosty margaritas, chilled beer, or wine are just right with this, followed by Tequila-Lime Grilled Shrimp (page 106) and Cuban Black Beans (page 143).

 IF YOU'RE NOT HAVING MARGARITAS OR WELL-CHILLED BEER, SOMETHING LIGHT AND FRIVOLOUS WOULD BE NICE HERE, SUCH AS AN OFF-DRY RIESLING, A CHENIN BLANC, OR A GEWÜRZTRAMINER.

1. Combine all the ingredients except the avocado in a medium bowl. Cover and refrigerate for 1 hour.

2. Spoon into a serving bowl. Just before serving, gently stir in the avocado and taste for seasoning. Garnish with cilantro leaves.

Advance Preparation: The salsa may be prepared up to 4 hours ahead through step 1 and refrigerated.

Note: When working with chilies, always wear rubber gloves. Wash the cutting surface and knife immediately afterward.

2 large tomatoes (about 1 pound), peeled, seeded, and finely diced

½ medium red sweet pepper, diced (about ½ cup)

½ medium yellow sweet pepper, diced (about ½ cup)

1 large carrot, peeled and diced (about ¾ cup)

½ cup corn kernels (from about 1 medium ear)

2 tablespoons finely chopped fresh cilantro

2 tablespoons finely chopped fresh Italian parsley

1 jalapeño chile, seeded and finely chopped (see note)

2 tablespoons fresh lemon juice

salt and freshly ground black pepper

1 medium avocado, pitted, peeled, and cut into ½-inch dice

Garnish

fresh cilantro leaves

with sweet mustard-basil sauce
basilgravlax

SERVES 8–12

Gravlax is usually prepared with dill, but this variation uses the stronger, more aromatic basil. The fish is actually cooked—or cured—by the marinade. You need to start this recipe 4 days before you plan to serve it, to allow time for the fish to cure properly. The mustard sauce has a consistency similar to mayonnaise. It's also good with sliced ham and poached salmon. Serve the gravlax with dark pumpernickel bread.

 A RIPE, CRISP, FRUITY CHARDONNAY WILL BRING OUT THE BASIL FLAVOR AND NEATLY BALANCE THE SALMON.

1. Lay the salmon on a sheet of waxed paper. Combine the sugar, salt, and white peppercorns in a small bowl. Sprinkle the salmon with half of the mixture. Turn and sprinkle the other side with the remaining mixture. Press down firmly on the salmon to coat it evenly with the seasonings.

2. Place 2 bunches of the basil on the bottom of a large, shallow nonaluminum pan. Place the salmon on top. Arrange the remaining 2 bunches of basil over the salmon. Cover tightly with aluminum foil or plastic wrap, place a weight on top (use a heavy pot lid, brick, or large can), and refrigerate.

3. Turn the salmon twice a day for 4 days. Make sure the basil and peppercorns remain evenly distributed.

4. To make the sauce, in a food processor or blender, combine the mustard, brown sugar, vinegar, and dry mustard and process for a few seconds. With the machine running, pour in the oil in a steady stream and process until thick and smooth. Pour into a small bowl, stir in the basil, and taste for seasoning. You should have about 1 cup. Cover and chill for at least 2 to 3 hours.

5. To serve, remove the basil and peppercorns. Lightly pat the salmon dry with a paper towel, making sure to remove all the salt and sugar. Slice paper-thin on the bias and arrange on a platter. Garnish with lemon wedges and basil leaves and serve with the sauce and dark pumpernickel bread.

Advance Preparation: The sauce may be prepared up to several weeks in advance, tightly covered, and refrigerated.

One 2½ to 3 pound salmon fillet

3 tablespoons sugar

2 tablespoons kosher or coarse salt

2 teaspoons white peppercorns

4 large bunches fresh basil

Sauce

¼ cup Dijon or whole-grain mustard

3 tablespoons dark brown sugar

2 tablespoons cider vinegar

1 teaspoon dry mustard

⅓ cup vegetable oil

3 tablespoons finely chopped
    fresh basil

Garnish

lemon wedges

fresh basil leaves

dark pumpernickel bread

The following is a list of raw vegetable possibilities to fill your basket or platter. If you are serving a wide variety of vegetables, allow about 2 ounces of each vegetable per person.

Thin asparagus, tough ends trimmed*

French green beans (haricots verts), trimmed, left whole*

Broccoli, cut into florets*

Green, purple, red, or yellow sweet peppers,
    seeded and cut into strips

Carrots, cut into sticks

Celery, peeled and cut into sticks

English cucumber, unpeeled, cut into sticks

Jicama, peeled and cut into sticks

Button mushrooms

White and red radishes

Snow peas, trimmed, left whole

Sugar snap peas, trimmed, left whole

Red and yellow round and/or pear-shaped cherry tomatoes

Zucchini, cut into sticks

*Immerse in boiling water for 1 minute and then chill.

crudités

Some sauce accompaniments

Tapenade mayonnaise (page 186)

Roasted Garlic Mayonnaise (page 186)

Buttermilk Dressing with Garden Herbs (page 183)

Tomato-Cucumber Salsa (page 191)

goatcheeseandpestotorta

SERVES 6–8

This torta is constructed by layering softened goat cheese, sliced hazelnuts, and pesto. I like to serve it as an hors d'oeuvre with crisp, thin plain crackers. Offer it as a prelude to Grilled Halibut in Lemon-Mustard-Tarragon Marinade (page 101) and your favorite grilled vegetables. For dessert offer a platter of fresh peaches, nectarines, and Toasted Almond Cookies with Lemon and Port (page 174).

 A FULL-BODIED CHARDONNAY COMPLEMENTS THIS TORTA, OR TRY A PARTICULARLY SPICY, YOUNG ZINFANDEL OR CHIANTI.

2 tablespoons sliced or
chopped hazelnuts

½ pound fresh goat cheese,
at room temperature

¼ pound cream cheese,
at room temperature

½ cup Spinach Pesto (page 192)

Garnish

large fresh red and green
basil leaves

sliced hazelnuts

toasted French bread or
water crackers

1. Preheat the oven to 350°F. Toast the hazelnuts until light brown, 3 to 5 minutes. Remove from the oven and let cool.

2. Oil a 3½-by-6-by-2½-inch loaf pan. Completely line the pan with plastic wrap, leaving enough overhang to fold over the top of the finished torta later and carefully tucking it into all the corners.

3. Combine the goat cheese and cream cheese in a food processor or bowl and process or beat until completely blended.

4. With a rubber spatula, spread half the softened cheese in an even layer on the bottom of the prepared pan. Sprinkle with 1 tablespoon of the hazelnuts. Carefully spoon the pesto on top, creating an even layer. Sprinkle with the remaining 1 tablespoon hazelnuts. With the rubber spatula, spread the remaining cheese mixture evenly over the top; the pesto should not show through.

5. Cover with the plastic wrap and refrigerate for at least 4 hours, or until well set.

6. To unmold, fold back the plastic wrap, lift the whole "package" from the pan, and invert onto a rectangular platter and peel off the plastic wrap. Use a paper towel to blot any excess pesto that has leaked down the sides of the torta. To garnish, press the basil leaves and hazelnuts into the sides. Serve with crackers or slices of freshly toasted French bread.

Advance Preparation: This may be prepared 1 day in advance through step 4 and refrigerated.

roasted eggplant
with balsamic vinegar

SERVES 6–8

Balsamic vinegar, the pride of Modena, is made from the boiled-down must of white Trebbiano grapes. It varies greatly in quality, so taste it before you cook with it. The older the vinegar, the more concentrated and full-bodied the flavor and the less you will need. ❋ *The sultry Mediterranean taste of this appetizer comes from its combination of deep flavors: balsamic vinegar, shallots, fresh basil, extra-virgin olive oil. The soft roasted eggplant absorbs these robust elements without losing its own unique taste. A border of roasted red peppers and Niçoise olives on the serving dish looks particularly attractive. Serve with Toasted Pita with Parmesan (page 42) or crisp crackers.*

 SERVE WITH A BARREL-FERMENTED CHARDONNAY.

1. Preheat the oven to 400°F.
2. Place the eggplant pieces in a large colander and sprinkle evenly with salt. Place over a bowl to drain for 30 minutes, tossing once or twice.
3. In a large roasting pan, stir together the shallots, garlic, vinegar, olive oil, and pepper.
4. Dry the eggplant pieces with paper towels. Place in the roasting pan and toss to coat evenly.
5. Place in the oven and roast, tossing with a large spoon every 15 minutes to ensure even cooking, until soft, about 45 minutes. Remove from the oven and let cool. Add the chopped basil and taste for seasoning.
6. Mound the eggplant on a serving dish. Garnish with the marinated red pepper slices, Niçoise olives, and basil leaves.

Advance Preparation: This may be prepared 1 day in advance through step 5 and refrigerated. Remove from the refrigerator 30 minutes before serving.

6 pounds eggplant (about 4 large),
   peeled and cut into
   ½-inch pieces
salt
6 medium shallots, finely chopped
2 medium garlic cloves, minced
½ cup balsamic vinegar
¼ cup extra-virgin olive oil
½ teaspoon freshly ground
   black pepper
leaves from 1 bunch fresh basil,
   finely chopped

Garnish
2 red sweet peppers, roasted (page
   196), seeded, peeled, cut
   lengthwise into strips ¼ inch
   wide and marinated in 2 tablespoons each olive oil and
   balsamic vinegar
16 Niçoise olives
fresh basil leaves

corn-leekcakes
with caviar, smoked salmon, and crème fraîche

MAKES ABOUT 32
SMALL PANCAKES;
SERVES 8

These delicate mini corn cakes look especially inviting on a large round platter decorated with watercress or dill sprigs and, if available, tiny white corn on the cob. They are the perfect way to start a formal dinner, such as Barbecued Leg of Lamb with a Mustard-Sage Crust (page 123) and Orzo with Goat Cheese (page 72). Finish the meal with Frozen Praline Mousse (page 173) with Bittersweet Hot Fudge Sauce (page 177).

 SERVE A SOFT, OFF-DRY JOHANNISBERG RIESLING OR A CRISP ALSATIAN WHITE. IF YOU ARE FEELING MORE FESTIVE, A SNAPPY BLANC DE BLANC OR BRUT CHAMPAGNE WOULD BE LOVELY.

1. Place the corn kernels in a food processor and pulse just until coarsely chopped. Set aside.

2. In a medium skillet over medium heat, melt ¼ cup of the butter. Pour off 2 tablespoons and reserve. Add the leeks to the skillet and sauté until softened, about 10 minutes. Set aside.

3. In a blender, combine the half-and-half, eggs, reserved melted butter, and salt and pepper to taste. Blend until mixed. Add the cornmeal and flour and blend until a smooth batter forms. Add the coarsely chopped corn and sautéed leeks and blend just until mixed.

4. Melt the remaining ¼ cup butter in a large nonstick skillet or on a griddle over medium heat.

5. Using a small ladle or measuring cup with a pouring spout, pour about 1 tablespoon of the batter into the skillet for each cake. Do not crowd the pan. Cook until the cakes bubble and are just set, about 2 minutes. Then flip the cakes and cook for another minute. Turn out onto a paper-towel-lined baking sheet to absorb any excess oil. Keep warm. Repeat until all are cooked.

6. To serve, place the cakes on a large serving platter and garnish each with a dollop of crème fraîche, caviar, a small piece of salmon, and a small sprig of watercress or dill. Serve immediately.

Advance Preparation: The batter may be made up to 1 day in advance and refrigerated. The corn cakes may be cooked up to 2 hours ahead and kept warm in a very slow oven. Remove the paper-towel liner before placing the cakes in the oven for reheating.

1 cup corn kernels (from about 2
    medium ears)
½ cup (1 stick) unsalted butter
2 medium leeks, white part only, very
    finely chopped
1 cup half-and-half
2 eggs
salt and freshly ground white pepper
½ cup fine yellow cornmeal
½ cup all-purpose flour

Garnish
½ cup crème fraîche
2 ounces caviar
2 ounces smoked salmon, cut into
    small pieces
fresh dill or watercress sprigs

Sparkling wine always seems to put people in a good mood. In warm weather, a chilled glass of bubbly can turn an ordinary meal into a special occasion. Americans have fallen in love with sparklers, and domestic wineries have obliged with a torrent of lively wines in every price category. A good sparkling wine generally costs about the same as a still wine, and it can usually be substituted when a white wine is appropriate.

Sparkling wine is best if chilled in an ice bucket, but if that is too cumbersome, half an hour in the refrigerator should do the trick. Champagne (a word that legitimately only applies to sparkling wines made in the Champagne district of France) and other sparklers should be served at 50°F to 55°F. The price of Champagne rises and falls with the dollar. When it's high, a good nonvintage Brut is affordable. Champagne is incomparable, but if you're willing to settle for something less extraordinary, look for a sparkling wine from other French regions or from Spain or Italy. All offer some good buys.

The perfect glass for sparkling wine is the flute or tulip. These slender, tall glasses preserve the bubbles, and the chimney shape neatly concentrates the wine's delightful perfume, allowing the aroma to be appreciated while the wine is sipped. The curiously popular saucer-shaped glass, on the other hand, totally defeats the purpose of the bubbles and dissipates the aroma. Too shallow to permit the bubbles to rise gracefully and too wide at the top, it allows both the bubbles and the aroma to escape too quickly. This awful glass can turn any sparkling wine flat in a very short time.

sparkling wine

stuffedbabyredpotatoes
with eggplant, tomato, and peppers

SERVES 6–8
AS AN
APPETIZER;
OR 10–12 AS
A SIDE DISH

Because they are easy to pick up and absorb the flavor of any filling, tiny new potatoes, the size of medium apricots, make great appetizers. This Provençal-inspired filling of peppers, tomatoes, and eggplant is classically robust. It is cooked until meltingly tender, creating a wonderful textural contrast with the crunchy potato shell.

 BALANCE THESE RICH FLAVORS WITH A FRUITY CHIANTI CLASSICO OR BEAUJOLAIS SERVED AT CELLAR TEMPERATURE (60°F).

1. Preheat the oven to 475°F.
2. To make the filling, in a large skillet over medium heat, warm the olive oil. Add the onion and sauté, stirring occasionally, until translucent, about 5 minutes.
3. Add the eggplant and continue cooking for 5 to 7 minutes.
4. Add the peppers and cook, stirring frequently, for 5 minutes longer.
5. Add the tomatoes, garlic, and basil and continue cooking, stirring occasionally, until slightly thickened, 5 to 10 minutes more. Season with salt and pepper. Set aside.
6. Meanwhile, prepare the potatoes: Place them on a baking sheet and bake for 35 to 45 minutes, depending on their size. They should be cooked through and slightly crispy. Remove from the oven and let cool.
7. Cut in half and scoop out the pulp, leaving a thin layer of potato in the skin. Brush the potato skins with the olive oil, turn upside down, and return to the oven until crisp, 10 to 15 minutes.
8. Remove from the oven, sprinkle the insides of the potatoes with some of the Parmesan cheese, and fill with the vegetable mixture. Sprinkle the tops with the remaining Parmesan cheese.
9. Reduce the oven to 425°F. Bake the potatoes until heated through, 10 to 15 minutes. Serve immediately.

Advance Preparation: The filling may be prepared up to 1 day ahead and refrigerated. Reheat gently before continuing.

Note: You will have extra filling, fortunately. It's delicious on pasta or chicken or used as a filling for crêpes or omelets.

Filling

2 tablespoons olive oil

1 small onion, very finely chopped

1 medium eggplant, peeled and cut into
½-inch dice

1 red sweet pepper, seeded and cut into
½-inch dice

1 yellow sweet pepper, seeded and cut
into ½-inch dice

1 green sweet pepper, seeded and cut
into ½-inch dice

2 pounds plum (Roma) tomatoes,
peeled, seeded, and finely chopped

2 medium garlic cloves, minced

2 tablespoons finely chopped fresh basil

salt and freshly ground black pepper

Potatoes

1½ pounds baby red potatoes
(16), unpeeled

2 tablespoons olive oil

½ cup freshly grated Parmesan cheese

spicygrilledporktenderloin

SERVES 4–6

These piquant brochettes were inspired by Thai satay, skewered meat or chicken grilled over a charcoal fire. Usually satay is served with a peanut sauce, but here a sour cream–based sauce marries the tang of citrus with the heat of hot-pepper oil for a summery barbecued appetizer.

 THIS DISH GOES NICELY WITH A MEDIUM TO HEAVYWEIGHT CHARDONNAY OR, IF YOU ARE FEELING DARING, TRY A YOUNG, SLIGHTLY CHILLED ZINFANDEL.

1. If using bamboo skewers, soak them in cold water for at least 30 minutes to prevent burning.
2. To make the marinade, in a bowl, whisk together all the ingredients. Pour off 3 tablespoons and reserve.
3. Skewer the pork. Place in a shallow nonaluminum dish. Pour the marinade over the skewers and marinate in the refrigerator for 6 to 12 hours.
4. In a small bowl, combine all the ingredients for the orange-cilantro cream, including the reserved marinade, and mix well. Taste for seasoning. Cover and refrigerate until ready to serve.
5. Prepare the barbecue for medium-heat grilling.
6. Remove the skewers from the marinade and grill about 3 inches from the fire, turning once, 4 to 7 minutes on each side, depending on the thickness of the meat. To test for doneness, cut into a piece of pork; it should be just cooked through.
7. Arrange the skewers on a large plate and garnish with cilantro leaves. Serve with the orange-cilantro cream.

Advance Preparation: The marinade and orange-cilantro cream may be prepared 1 day in advance and refrigerated.

Marinade

½ cup fresh orange juice

2 tablespoons fresh lime juice

1 teaspoon chopped fresh oregano

1 teaspoon finely chopped
    fresh cilantro

1 teaspoon chopped fresh marjoram

¼ teaspoon ground cumin

2 tablespoons vegetable oil

salt and freshly ground black pepper

1 pound pork tenderloin, cut into
    1-inch pieces or thin horizontal
    slices while partially frozen

Orange-Cilantro Cream

½ cup sour cream

finely chopped zest of 1 orange

2 tablespoons finely chopped
    fresh cilantro

1 teaspoon hot-pepper oil, or to taste

3 tablespoons reserved marinade

Garnish

fresh cilantro leaves

herbedgarliccheesebread

SERVES 8

This is the perfect accompaniment to many barbecued dishes. It's also a nice way to begin your evening while awaiting dinner. Using freshly grated Parmesan cheese makes this version of the American classic a standout. Try it with Pasta Shells with Peppers, Mushrooms, and Sausages (page 65) or Grilled Whole Bluefish with Lemon-Dill Butter (page 109).

1. Preheat oven to 400°F.

2. In a small bowl, combine the butter, garlic, ¼ cup of the Parmesan cheese, the basil, thyme, oregano, and salt and pepper to taste. Mix until well blended.

3. Slice the bread in half lengthwise and spread the cut side of each half with half of the butter mixture. Sprinkle with the remaining Parmesan cheese. Slice the bread halves into 2-inch-thick slices about three-fourths of the way through. Make sure that you haven't cut all the way through, and that the crust is still holding the bread together. Wrap each half tightly in aluminum foil.

4. Place the loaves on a baking sheet and bake for 10 to 15 minutes. The topping should be bubbling. Remove from the foil wrap and serve immediately.

Advance Preparation: This may be prepared 4 hours in advance through step 3 and refrigerated. Remove from the refrigerator 30 minutes before baking.

½ cup (1 stick) unsalted butter, at
    room temperature

3 medium garlic cloves, minced

½ cup freshly grated
    Parmesan cheese

1 tablespoon finely chopped
    fresh basil

½ teaspoon finely chopped
    fresh thyme

¼ teaspoon fresh oregano leaves, or
    pinch of dried oregano

salt and freshly ground white pepper

1 large loaf French or sourdough
    French bread

with parmesan
toasted pita

SERVES 4–6

These tasty pita triangles are versatile and easy to make. Serve them in a pretty basket lined with a colorful napkin all by themselves with a glass of wine. They are also great offered alongside Roasted Eggplant with Balsamic Vinegar (page 35), Golden Summer Soup (page 44), or Chicken Salad with Roasted Garlic Mayonnaise (page 91).

1. Preheat the broiler.

2. Using a knife, slit each pita along the seam and then separate into 2 rounds. Put the halves together again, and cut each round into 8 triangles. Arrange the triangles on a baking sheet, crust side down.

3. Brush the triangles with the olive oil and sprinkle them with the Parmesan cheese.

4. Broil until golden, 3 to 4 minutes. Serve hot.

2 medium rounds pita bread, sesame or plain

2 tablespoons olive oil

2 tablespoons freshly grated Parmesan cheese

Advance Preparation: These may be prepared 8 hours in advance and served at room temperature.

☀ no-time appetizers

Smoked salmon with capers, lemon wedges, and softened unsalted butter on thin toast.

Belgian endive leaves spread or piped with a mixture of blue cheese and cream cheese and garnished with bay shrimp.

Icy-cold red and white radishes with coarse salt and unsalted butter.

Chilled shrimp with Summer Vinaigrette (page 182).

Smoked oysters on a bed of lettuce with sauce of sour cream, minced fresh dill, and fresh lemon juice.

Slices of melon or wedges of fig wrapped in prosciutto.

soups

goldensummersoup

In the past few years, yellow produce—yellow pear and cherry tomatoes, yellow zucchini, yellow beets, yellow raspberries, and even yellow watermelon—has become a mainstay at farmers' markets and greengrocers. These sunny gems are considerably less acidic than their red counterparts. ✳ This soup, with its just-picked corn, yellow sweet peppers, and yellow cherry tomatoes, looks and tastes like pure summertime. If you can't find yellow tomatoes, use the red variety and red sweet peppers for an equally delicious variation. A touch of hot-pepper oil gives it extra zing. Serve the soup as a first course in attractive pottery cups or small glass bowls for an outdoor luncheon. Follow with cold Roasted Rosemary-Lemon Chicken (page 118) and Cracked Wheat–Vegetable Salad (page 86). Finish with Hazelnut-Plum Tart (page 169) topped with crème fraîche.

1. In a large saucepan over medium heat, warm the olive oil. Add the scallions and sauté until slightly softened, about 3 minutes.

2. Reserve ¼ cup corn, ¼ cup chopped tomatoes, and 2 tablespoons diced yellow pepper. Add the remaining corn, tomatoes, and yellow pepper to the pan and sauté until slightly softened, about 3 minutes.

3. Add the chicken stock and basil, increase the heat to medium-high and bring to a boil. Reduce the heat to medium-low and simmer slowly, uncovered, for about 10 minutes. Remove and discard the basil leaves.

4. Puree the soup in the pan with a hand blender or in batches in a blender or food processor. Pass through a food mill placed over a bowl, or pour through a sieve, pressing against the solids to extract all of the essence.

5. Stir in the cream, salt and pepper to taste, and the hot-pepper oil. Taste for seasoning. Let cool, cover, and chill for at least 3 hours.

6. Immerse the reserved corn and yellow pepper in boiling water for about 2 minutes. Drain, let cool, cover, and chill.

7. To serve, taste the soup for seasoning. Ladle into bowls and garnish with the sour cream, chopped basil, and the reserved tomatoes, yellow pepper, and corn.

Advance Preparation: The soup and garnish may be prepared 1 day in advance through step 6 and refrigerated until serving.

3 tablespoons olive oil

6 scallions, white part only, finely chopped

2 cups corn kernels (from about 4 ears)

1 pint yellow cherry tomatoes, coarsely chopped

1 yellow sweet pepper, seeded and cut into ½-inch dice

6 cups chicken stock

6 fresh basil leaves

¼ cup whipping cream

salt and freshly ground black pepper

1 teaspoon hot-pepper oil

Garnish

½ cup sour cream

finely chopped fresh basil

mintedchinesesnowpeasoup

Mint and peas seem made for each other. While peas are often thought of as a springtime vegetable, they are lovely in the summer as well. I've added Chinese snow peas to sweeten and enliven the taste of the English peas. This versatile soup tastes good hot or cold. Served steaming hot on a cool evening, it is a wonderful opener for Light Summer Pasta (page 66) on a vegetarian menu. Chilled, it can precede Chicken Salad Niçoise (page 93).

1. In a large saucepan over medium heat, warm the olive oil. Add the scallions and carrot and sauté, stirring occasionally, until slightly softened, 3 to 5 minutes.

2. Add the lettuce and sauté until wilted, about 5 minutes.

3. Add the mint, chicken stock, all but a small handful of the snow peas, and the peas (if using thawed peas, add during the last 5 minutes). Cover and simmer over low heat until the vegetables are softened, about 20 minutes.

4. In blender or food processor, process the soup, in batches, until pureed. Return to the pan and add the cream, salt and pepper to taste, and the lemon juice. Bring to a simmer over medium-low heat and cook for about 5 minutes to blend the flavors. Taste for seasoning.

5. Refrigerate the soup until chilled, about 3 hours.

6. Slice the reserved snow peas in julienne and immerse in boiling water until slightly softened, about 1 minute. Drain, let cool, cover, and chill.

7. To serve, taste the soup for seasoning. Ladle into bowls and garnish with the sour cream, mint, scallion, and julienned snow peas.

Advance Preparation: This may be prepared 8 hours in advance through step 6 and refrigerated until serving.

2 tablespoons olive oil

6 scallions, white part only, finely chopped

1 large carrot, peeled and finely diced

1 head limestone or butter lettuce, leaves separated

3 tablespoons coarsely chopped fresh mint

4 cups chicken or vegetable stock

½ pound (about 1 cup) snow peas, trimmed

1 cup shelled fresh English peas (about 1 pound unshelled) or thawed frozen petite peas

2 tablespoons whipping cream or half-and-half

salt and freshly ground white pepper

1 tablespoon fresh lemon juice

Garnish

¼ cup sour cream

1 tablespoon finely chopped fresh mint

1 tablespoon finely chopped scallion, green part only

The popular soup and sandwich combination is a perfect answer to light summer eating. Select your favorite soup and accompany it with one of these suggestions. These sandwiches require excellent fresh bread or rolls and the best ingredients on hand:

- *Grilled sharp cheddar cheese, bacon, and tomato, spread with basil shallot mayonnaise (page 186), open faced on whole wheat or pumpernickel*
- *Cold marinated sliced flank steak and arugula leaves on sourdough rolls spread with ancho chile mayonnaise (page 186)*
- *Prosciutto, tomatoes, and roasted peppers spread with Roasted Garlic Mayonnaise (page 186) on sesame seed bread*
- *Chopped smoked salmon and egg salad on rye bread*
- *Smoked turkey slices, sliced tomatoes, red onion slices, basil, chervil or burnet leaves spread with lemon-chive mayonnaise (page 186) on whole wheat bread*
- *Cold grilled chicken slices, sliced avocado, and Tomato-Cucumber Salsa (page 191) stuffed in warm sesame pita bread*
- *Fresh goat cheese, marinated sun-dried tomatoes, and roasted red and yellow peppers on a sourdough roll spread with Roasted Garlic Mayonnaise (page 186)*

soup and sandwich combinations

yellowsquashsoup

Nearly any table will be brightened by this sunny yellow soup. And it cheers the cook, too, since it can be put together in just a few minutes. Follow with Chicken Salad with Roasted Garlic Mayonnaise (page 91) and Green Bean Salad with Yellow Pepper, Jicama, and Tomato (page 83).

1. In a saucepan over medium heat, warm the olive oil. Add the squash and chives and sauté until just softened, about 3 minutes.
2. Add the chicken stock and simmer, uncovered, for about 5 minutes.
3. In a blender or food processor, process the soup, in batches, until pureed. Cover and refrigerate until chilled, at least 3 hours.
4. Whisk in the sour cream, lemon juice, and salt and pepper to taste until well blended.
5. To serve, ladle the soup into bowls and garnish with the sour cream and chives.

Advance Preparation: This may be prepared 1 day in advance through step 4 and refrigerated until serving.

1 tablespoon olive oil

1½ pounds yellow crookneck
squashes, shredded

2 tablespoons finely chopped
fresh chives

3½ cups chicken stock

½ cup sour cream

1 tablespoon fresh lemon juice

salt and freshly ground white pepper

Garnish

¼ cup sour cream

1 tablespoon finely chopped
fresh chives

Every summer has its dog days—those stifling times when there's no breeze anywhere and the only hope of comfort is to sit absolutely still. If you have company coming, the very thought of cooking is unbearable. Here are some suggestions for serving cool, delicious food, with a minimum of effort. Remember to go light on alcoholic drinks, as it's easy to drink too fast when the sun is bright.

Drinks —

Wines, beers, and refreshing mixed drinks
Icy-cold sparkling mineral water with lime wedges
Fruit nectars mixed with sparkling water

First Courses —

Deviled eggs (page 62)
Crudités (page 33) with Guacamole Salsa (page 30)
Goat Cheese and Pesto Torta with Hazelnuts (page 34)
Chilled cracked crab with lemon-chive mayonnaise

Main Courses —

A platter of sardines, sliced tomatoes,
 hard-cooked eggs, and olives
A variety of sliced melons and Black Forest ham
 or prosciutto
Halved hard-cooked eggs with Summer Vinaigrette
 (page 182), roasted sweet peppers with balsamic
 vinegar, Niçoise olives, and crusty French bread
Mixed greens with chopped shrimp and tomatoes

Desserts —

Ice cream or sorbet
Fresh berries with mint leaves
Cheese and fruit platter with assorted tea breads or cookies

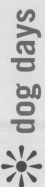

dog days

creamy gazpacho

SERVES 6–8

I first tasted this light and creamy soup at the Château San Martin in the hills of southern France, overlooking the Mediterranean. The setting was as memorable as the gazpacho, which the chef serves daily during the hot summer months. The anchovy paste and crème fraîche add an unanticipated complexity. For a variation, I like to puree a few cups of the soup and stir it into the remaining soup for textural interest.

1. In a large bowl, stir the anchovy paste into the tomato juice until dissolved. Add the chopped tomatoes, chicken stock, olive oil, vinegar, garlic, and salt and pepper to taste. Whisk together until well blended.

2. Add the cucumbers, onion, and basil to the soup mixture. Reserve 2 tablespoons each of the chopped red and yellow peppers for the garnish. Stir the remaining peppers into the soup. Cover and refrigerate until chilled, at least 4 hours.

3. Just before serving, in a small bowl, whisk the sour cream with 1 cup of the soup mixture until completely blended. Add to the remaining soup and whisk vigorously. Taste for seasoning.

4. To serve, ladle the soup into bowls and garnish with the reserved chopped red and yellow pepper, sour cream, and basil.

Advance Preparation: This may be prepared 8 hours in advance through step 2 and refrigerated until serving.

2 teaspoons anchovy paste

3 cups tomato juice

2½ pounds ripe tomatoes, peeled, seeded, and finely chopped

2 cups chicken stock

2 tablespoons extra-virgin olive oil

3 tablespoons red wine vinegar

3 large garlic cloves, minced

salt and freshly ground black pepper

2 cucumbers, peeled, seeded, and finely chopped

3 tablespoons very finely chopped red onion

¼ cup finely chopped fresh basil

1 small red sweet pepper, seeded and very finely chopped

1 small yellow sweet pepper, seeded and very finely chopped

¼ cup sour cream or crème fraîche

Garnish

½ cup sour cream or crème fraîche

2 tablespoons finely chopped fresh basil

chilled avocado soup
with tomato-cucumber salsa

SERVES 4

The ideal summer soup doesn't require cooking. This cool, refreshing option is amazingly simple, as all you need is a food processor or a blender. The crisp, chunky Tomato-Cucumber Salsa (page 191) spooned on top creates a striking color contrast. Serve the soup with your favorite chopped vegetable salad. Together they make an easy, light meal that will keep you out of the kitchen on a hot August day.

1. Pit and peel the avocados and cut into large pieces. Place in a food processor or blender and process until pureed.
2. Add the chicken stock, lemon juice, chives, chili powder, and salt to taste, and process until smooth. Taste for seasoning. Cover and refrigerate until chilled, at least 4 hours.
3. To serve, ladle the soup into bowls and garnish with a dollop each of sour cream and Tomato-Cucumber Salsa.

Advance Preparation: This may be prepared 8 hours in advance through step 2 and refrigerated until serving.

2 large, ripe avocados

3 cups chicken stock

2 tablespoons fresh lemon juice

2 tablespoons finely chopped
  fresh chives

½ teaspoon chili powder

salt

Garnish

¼ cup sour cream

½ cup Tomato-Cucumber Salsa
  (page 191)

with carrots, cucumbers, and sour cream
coldbeetsoup

SERVES 8–10

This is a far cry from the bottled borscht I grew up on. Sweet julienned carrot and refreshing cucumber added just before serving give it extra crunch. I like to serve the soup in oversized glass balloon goblets for a dramatic presentation. Follow with Scallops Brochette with Spicy Caribbean Salsa (page 98) and Lemon-Herb Roasted Potatoes (page 152).

1. In a large nonaluminum soup pot, combine the beets, chicken stock, white wine, and sugar. Bring to a boil over medium-high heat, reduce the heat to medium, cover, and simmer until the beets are tender, 30 to 40 minutes.

2. Using a slotted spoon, transfer the beets to a bowl and let cool. When cool enough to be handled, peel and cut into julienne strips. Cover and chill.

3. Strain the stock through a fine-mesh sieve lined with cheesecloth into a large bowl. Cover and refrigerate until chilled, at least 4 hours.

4. Blanch the carrots in a saucepan of boiling salted water for about 1 minute. Drain in a colander and run under cold water to stop the cooking. Drain, cover, and chill.

5. When ready to serve, skim the fat from the surface of the chilled stock and discard. Add the beets, carrots, cucumbers, dill, lemon juice, vinegar, and salt and pepper to taste. Mix well. Taste for seasoning.

6. To serve, ladle into bowls and garnish with the sour cream and dill.

Advance Preparation: This may be prepared 1 day in advance through step 5 and refrigerated until serving.

---

2 pounds beets, well scrubbed and trimmed with roots and ½ inch of the stems attached

2 quarts chicken stock

1½ cups dry white wine

1 tablespoon plus 1 teaspoon sugar

2 medium carrots, peeled and julienned

2 medium cucumbers, peeled, seeded, and julienned

2 tablespoons finely chopped fresh dill

2 tablespoons fresh lemon juice

2 tablespoons red wine vinegar

salt and freshly ground black pepper

Garnish

1 cup sour cream

2 tablespoons finely chopped fresh dill

spinach**vichyssoise**

Fresh watercress and spinach brighten this classic summer soup. A finishing dollop of lemony cream brings out its tangy flavor. This is a hearty dish, so serve small portions, or consider it for a light main dish accompanied with Herbed Garlic Cheese Bread (page 41). It is also excellent served hot.

1. In a soup pot over medium heat, warm the vegetable oil. Add the leeks and sauté, stirring occasionally, until softened, about 5 minutes. Add the potatoes and continue sautéing until the potatoes are slightly softened, about 5 minutes. Add the spinach and watercress and sauté until wilted, about 3 minutes.
2. Increase the heat to medium-high. Add the chicken stock and bring to a boil. Reduce to medium-low, cover partially, and cook until the vegetables are tender, about 15 minutes.
3. Puree the soup until smooth in the pot with a hand blender or in batches in a blender or food processor. Pour into a large bowl and add salt and pepper to taste, and the lemon juice. Taste for seasoning. Cover and refrigerate until well chilled, for at least 4 hours.
4. To make the lemon-chive cream, combine all the ingredients in a small bowl and mix well.
5. To serve, ladle the soup into bowls and garnish each with a dollop of the lemon-chive cream.

Advance Preparation: The soup may be prepared 1 day in advance through step 3 and refrigerated until serving.

3 tablespoons vegetable oil

3 leeks, white and light green part only, coarsely chopped

1½ pounds White Rose potatoes, peeled and coarsely chopped

1 large bunch spinach, stemmed

1 medium bunch watercress, stemmed

2 quarts chicken stock

salt and freshly ground white pepper

1 tablespoon fresh lemon juice

Lemon-Chive Cream

½ cup sour cream

2 tablespoons fresh lemon juice

1 tablespoon finely chopped fresh chives

cornchowder

SERVES 6

Every summer includes a few chilly days when you crave something warm and substantial. This soup is a good solution because it uses seasonal produce in a hearty way. Serve big bowls of this chowder with hot, crusty French bread and Garden Salad with Goat Cheese–Thyme Dressing (page 80). Summer Fruit Compote (page 158) and Toasted Almond Cookies with Lemon and Port (page 174) make a satisfying finale.

1. Place the bacon pieces in a large nonaluminum soup pot over medium heat. Sauté until crisp and light brown, about 5 minutes. Using a slotted spoon, transfer to paper towels and reserve.
2. Add the onion to the bacon drippings over medium heat and sauté until softened but not browned, 3 to 5 minutes. Add the potatoes and sauté until slightly softened, about 3 minutes. Add the red pepper and continue to sauté for another minute, stirring constantly.
3. Raise the heat to medium-high, add the chicken stock and thyme, and bring to a boil. Reduce the heat to medium-low, cover partially, and simmer until the potatoes are just tender, about 20 minutes. Discard the thyme sprigs.
4. Scoop out about one-fourth of the potato-vegetable mixture and place in a food processor or blender. Process until smooth. Return the puree to the soup.
5. Add the corn and cream and cook for about 5 minutes longer to cook the corn and blend the flavors. Stir in the salt and pepper to taste.
6. Ladle into bowls and serve immediately.

Advance Preparation: This may be prepared 8 hours in advance through step 5 and refrigerated. Reheat gently before serving.

¼ pound bacon, cut into
    ½-inch pieces

1 large onion, finely chopped

2 pounds White Rose or Red Rose
    potatoes, peeled and cut into
    ½-inch pieces

1 large red sweet pepper, seeded
    and finely diced

6 cups chicken stock

2 fresh thyme sprigs

4 cups corn kernels (from about 8
    medium ears)

½ cup milk or whipping cream

salt and freshly ground white pepper

minestrone

with pesto cream

SERVES 6–8

Although this soup can be served hot, I prefer it at room temperature, which brings out the full flavor of the vegetables and herbs. Offer the soup as a simple, yet elegant first course before Barbecued Leg of Lamb with a Mustard-Sage Crust (page 123) and Herbed New Potatoes with Vermouth (page 154).

1. In a large soup pot over medium heat, warm the olive oil. Add the onions and sauté, stirring occasionally, until softened, 3 to 5 minutes.
2. Add the carrots, potatoes, zucchini, crookneck squash, and eggplant and sauté until slightly softened, about 3 minutes. Add the cabbage and sauté just until softened, about 3 minutes longer.
3. Raise the heat to medium-high, add the tomatoes, chicken stock, garlic, basil, and salt and pepper to taste, and bring to a boil. Reduce the heat to medium-low and simmer, uncovered, until the vegetables are tender, about 25 minutes. The soup will be slightly thickened.
4. Fill a separate saucepan three-fourths full of water and bring to a boil. Add the orzo and cook just until al dente, about 10 minutes. Drain and add to the soup. Add the white beans, stir, and taste for seasoning. Let cool to room temperature.
5. To make the pesto cream, combine all the ingredients in a small bowl, including salt and pepper to taste, and whisk until smooth. Cover and refrigerate.
6. To serve, ladle the soup into bowls and swirl a tablespoon of the pesto cream into each serving.

Advance Preparation: The soup and pesto cream may be prepared 1 day in advance and refrigerated. Bring both to room temperature before serving.

2 tablespoons olive oil

2 medium onions, finely chopped

4 medium carrots, peeled and cut into ¼-inch pieces

½ pound White Rose or Red Rose potatoes, peeled and cut into ¼-inch pieces

1 large zucchini, cut into ¼-inch pieces

1 large yellow crookneck squash, cut into ¼-inch pieces

1 Japanese eggplant or ½ small globe eggplant, cut into ¼-inch pieces

½ small cabbage, shredded

1 cup peeled, seeded, and pureed tomatoes

6 cups chicken stock

2 medium garlic cloves, minced

1 tablespoon finely chopped fresh basil

salt and freshly ground black pepper

¼ cup orzo

1 cup well-drained canned white beans

Spinach Pesto Cream

¼ cup Spinach Pesto (page 192)

2 teaspoons red wine vinegar

¼ cup crème fraîche

salt and freshly ground black pepper

toasted triangle crisps

Cut tortillas (corn or flour) or single-layer rounds of pita bread (split pita into 2 rounds along the seam) into 6 to 8 triangles. Top with one of the following and slip under the broiler just until golden brown.

- *Spread with Roasted Garlic Mayonnaise (page 186) and sprinkle freshly grated Parmesan cheese on top.*
- *Spread with basil-shallot mayonnaise (page 186) and sprinkle grated aged goat cheese on top.*
- *Brush with olive oil and sprinkle with crumbled fresh goat cheese and finely chopped fresh thyme.*
- *Spread with ancho chile mayonnaise (page 186).*
- *Brush with melted unsalted butter, chopped fresh herbs, salt, and freshly ground black pepper.*

lightentrées:
eggs, pasta, and pizza

summertime**frittata**

The classic Italian frittata looks like a big, yellow pancake, although it's actually a flat, round omelet cooked over low heat until firm. This version has sausages, zucchini, mushrooms, and plum tomatoes tucked inside, and it's decorated with dollops of sour cream and shredded basil. Frittatas can be eaten warm or at room temperature and served for brunch, lunch, or supper. Serve the frittata with Lemon-Herb Roasted Potatoes (page 152) and finish with Raspberry Pound Cake (page 163) and iced coffee.

 SERVE A SNAPPY, YOUNG RED SUCH AS GAMAY, ZINFANDEL, BARDOLINO, OR BEAUJOLAIS.

1. In a medium skillet over medium heat, cook the sausage, turning frequently until browned, about 10 minutes. Drain on paper towels and let cool. Cut into ¼-inch-thick slices and set aside.
2. Preheat the oven to 425°F.
3. In a medium bowl, whisk together the eggs, ½ teaspoon of the salt, and ⅛ teaspoon of the pepper. Stir in 1¼ cups of the cheese. Set aside.
4. In an ovenproof nonstick 12-inch skillet over medium-high heat, melt the butter with the olive oil. Add the shallots and sauté until softened but not brown, about 3 minutes. Add the mushrooms and sauté for 1 to 2 minutes. Add the zucchini and continue cooking for 2 minutes. Add the garlic and sauté for 1 minute. Arrange the sausage slices around the vegetables and season with the remaining ¼ teaspoon salt and ⅛ teaspoon pepper.
5. Pour the egg mixture over the sausages and vegetables and cook over medium-low heat, stirring occasionally, until lightly browned on the bottom, about 5 minutes. Arrange the sliced tomatoes around the edge of the skillet. Sprinkle with the remaining ¼ cup cheese.
6. Transfer the skillet to the oven and bake until the frittata is puffed and brown, 10 to 15 minutes.
7. Remove from the oven and invert onto a plate. Invert again onto a serving platter, so the tomato border faces up. (Alternatively, serve directly from the pan.) Place the sour cream in a large dollop in the center and garnish with the basil. Serve immediately.

2 sweet Italian sausages (⅓ to ½ pound total)

2 hot Italian sausages (⅓ to ½ pound total)

12 eggs

¾ teaspoon salt

¼ teaspoon freshly ground black pepper

1½ cups shredded sharp Cheddar cheese (about 6 ounces)

2 tablespoons unsalted butter

1 tablespoon olive oil

2 medium shallots, finely chopped

½ pound fresh mushrooms, thinly sliced

2 small zucchini, thinly sliced

1 medium garlic clove, minced

4 medium plum (Roma) tomatoes, sliced

recipe continues ▶

Advance Preparation: This may be prepared up to 2 hours in advance through step 4, omitting step 2, and kept covered at room temperature. Although it will be completely different in texture and taste, the frittata may also be made 1 day ahead, refrigerated, and served at room temperature.

deviled eggs

Deviled eggs, the beloved American classic, can be far from ordinary when sophisticated ingredients are added. The key to perfect deviled eggs is in the cooking: don't boil the eggs and don't cook them too long. These strategies will avoid tough eggs and those unappetizing gray circles around the yolks. Use extra-large eggs, preferably at room temperature. Place them in a saucepan with cold water to cover and bring just to a rolling boil. Turn off the heat, cover the pan, and let stand for 12 minutes. Cool the eggs under cold running water. Crack, but don't peel them until right before stuffing.

A few excellent combinations to mix with the mashed yolks are:

Chopped smoked salmon, snipped fresh chives, mayonnaise, and fresh lemon juice

Minced shallots, mayonnaise, and snipped fresh dill; top with caviar

Mayonnaise, mango chutney, and curry powder

Pesto, mayonnaise, and chopped bay shrimp

Yogurt, sour cream, chopped cucumber, and capers; garnish with watercress

Saffron mayonnaise with chopped fresh Italian parsley

with three cheeses
scrambled eggs

SERVES 4-6

On those lazy mornings when you want something absolutely delicious for breakfast, this luxurious scrambled-egg dish with diced tomatoes is the thing to cook. The eggs and Parmesan cheese are stirred constantly over low heat to produce a wonderfully creamy finish. The other cheeses are barely melted into the eggs. The tomatoes are added off the heat to preserve their texture. Decorate the serving plates with crisp triangular croutons and sprigs of fresh rosemary, basil, or parsley. Serve with bacon and a large platter of mixed fruits.

1. To make the croutons, cut each bread slice into 2 triangles. In a medium skillet over medium heat, melt the butter with the olive oil. Add the triangles, in batches, and brown on both sides, about 4 minutes total. With a spatula, transfer to paper towels to drain.
2. In a bowl, whisk together the eggs, Parmesan cheese, salt, and pepper.
3. In a medium-size heavy saucepan over low heat, melt 2 tablespoons of the butter. Add the egg mixture and cook over low heat, whisking constantly, until the mixture is thick but not dry. Remove from the heat and stir in the remaining 2 tablespoons butter and the Cheddar and mozzarella cheeses. Gently stir in the diced tomatoes. Taste for seasoning.
4. Transfer the egg mixture to a serving bowl. Stick one corner of each crouton into the egg mixture at the edge of the bowl. Serve immediately.

Croutons

3 square slices firm white bread,
  crusts trimmed
1 tablespoon unsalted butter
1½ tablespoons olive oil

12 eggs
2 tablespoons freshly grated
  Parmesan cheese
½ teaspoon salt
¼ teaspoon freshly ground
  black pepper
¼ cup (½ stick) unsalted butter
½ cup shredded Cheddar cheese
½ cup shredded mozzarella cheese
2 firm, yet ripe tomatoes, peeled,
  seeded, and diced

with zucchini, tomato, and basil
omelet

SERVES 6

This is my favorite summer omelet, perfect for an informal, everyone-in-the-kitchen meal. I prepare the filling ahead of time and make the omelets at the last minute, using two skillets. Serve chilled Champagne with framboise when your guests arrive. Accompany the omelets with Herbed New Potatoes with Vermouth (page 154) or Lemon-Herb Roasted Potatoes (page 152). For dessert serve Poached Peaches in White Zinfandel with Raspberry Sauce (page 156) and Toasted Almond Cookies with Lemon and Port (page 174).

1. To make the filling, in a medium skillet over medium heat, melt the butter. Add the shallot and sauté until softened, about 2 minutes. Add the mushrooms and sauté until softened, about 2 minutes. Add the zucchini and continue to sauté for 2 minutes.

2. Add the tomato, raise the heat to high, and cook for 2 minutes to evaporate any excess liquid from the tomato. Season with salt and pepper, and stir in the basil. Taste for seasoning. Cover to keep warm.

3. To prepare each omelet, in a small bowl whisk together 2 or 3 eggs, a pinch of salt, a pinch of pepper, and ½ teaspoon club soda until smooth.

4. In an 8-inch omelet pan or skillet over medium heat, melt 1 tablespoon butter until it begins to sizzle. Pour in the egg mixture and stir the center with the flat side of a fork. With the prongs of the fork, lift the edges of the omelet so any uncooked mixture runs to the edge of the pan. Vigorously slide the pan back and forth over the heat until the omelet begins to slip around freely.

5. When the omelet is lightly cooked but still creamy in the center, spoon about 2 tablespoons of the filling over the half closest to the pan's handle. Sprinkle 1 tablespoon of the Parmesan cheese over the filling.

6. Using the handle, quickly jerk the pan toward you so that the uncovered half of the omelet flips over to cover the filling. Slide the folded omelet onto a serving dish. Serve immediately or keep warm in a low oven while preparing the remaining omelets.

Advance Preparation: The filling may be prepared 1 day in advance without the basil and refrigerated. Remove it from the refrigerator 30 minutes before using, add the basil, and reheat gently.

Filling

2 tablespoons unsalted butter

1 shallot, minced

¼ pound fresh mushrooms,
    thinly sliced

1 medium zucchini, julienned

1 medium tomato, peeled, seeded,
    and coarsely chopped

salt and freshly ground black pepper

2 tablespoons chopped fresh basil

6 tablespoons freshly grated
    Parmesan cheese

Omelets

12 to 18 eggs (2 or 3 per person)

Salt and freshly ground pepper

1 tablespoon club soda

6 tablespoons (¾ stick)
    unsalted butter

pasta shells
with peppers, mushrooms, and sausages

SERVES 6–8

Pasta shells are pretty to look at and easy to eat. Sautéed vegetables simmered in port and stock reduce to form a light sauce, while grilled sausages add enough substance to make this a satisfying main course. You can find sweet and hot sausages at most Italian grocery stores, where they often make their own. Begin this meal with Goat Cheese and Pesto Torta with Hazelnuts (page 34) and crisp crackers. Serve with a simple mixed green salad with Summer Vinaigrette (page 182). Finish with Poached Peaches in White Zinfandel with Raspberry Sauce (page 156).

 SERVE A MEDIUM-WEIGHT ZINFANDEL OR A RED FROM THE RHÔNE VALLEY.

1. Prepare the barbecue for medium-high-heat grilling.
2. Grill the sausages about 4 inches from the fire, turning as needed, until the juices run clear, about 20 minutes. (Alternatively, cook the sausages in a preheated broiler.) Transfer to a platter and let cool.
3. In a large, deep skillet over medium heat, melt 1 tablespoon each of the butter and olive oil. Add the peppers and sauté until just slightly softened, about 3 minutes. Transfer to a bowl.
4. Add the remaining 2 tablespoons butter and 1 tablespoon to the skillet. When the butter melts, add the shallots and mushrooms and sauté, stirring occasionally, until softened, 3 to 5 minutes. Transfer to the bowl holding the peppers.
5. Add the stock, cream, and port and bring to a simmer. Cook until very slightly thickened. Add the peppers, shallots, mushrooms, parsley, and salt and pepper to taste.
6. Cut the sausages on the diagonal into 1¼-inch-thick slices and add to the sauce. Keep warm.
7. Meanwhile, bring a large pot of water to a boil. Add the 1 teaspoon salt and the pasta, stir well, and boil until al dente, 7 to 10 minutes. Drain well and place in a large serving bowl.
8. Pour the sauce over the pasta and mix well. Garnish with the parsley and a few tablespoons of the Parmesan cheese. Serve immediately. Pass the remaining cheese at the table.

Advance Preparation: This may be prepared 4 hours in advance through step 6 and refrigerated. Reheat the sauce gently.

1 pound sweet Italian sausages

1 pound hot Italian sausages

3 tablespoons unsalted butter

2 tablespoons olive oil

1 large red sweet pepper, seeded and cut lengthwise into ¼-inch strips

1 large yellow sweet pepper, seeded and cut lengthewise into ¼-inch strips

4 medium shallots, finely chopped

1 pound fresh mushrooms, sliced

2 cups veal or chicken stock

¾ cup whipping cream

½ cup tawny port

1 tablespoon finely chopped fresh parsley

Salt to taste, plus 1 teaspoon

Freshly ground white pepper

1½ pounds pasta shells

Garnish

1 tablespoon finely chopped fresh parsley

1 cup freshly grated Parmesan cheese

lightsummerpasta

SERVES 4-6

One night a friend and I decided to come up with some no-cook pasta sauces. The friend happened to be Leslie Margolis, a great cook who specializes in light cuisine. We got so carried away we made several sauces and invited other confirmed pasta lovers to choose the best one. This sauce was the winner. The only cooking required is for the pasta, which leaves you plenty of time to enjoy your company.

1. In a serving bowl, combine the tomatoes, olive oil, basil, parsley, garlic, mozzarella cheese, and ¼ cup of the Parmesan cheese. Mix well. Season with salt and pepper and mix well again.

2. Bring a large pot of water to a boil. Add the 1 teaspoon salt and the pasta, stir well, and boil until al dente, 8 to 10 minutes. Drain well and place the pasta over the sauce.

3. Toss the pasta with the sauce. Garnish with basil leaves and pass the remaining ¼ cup Parmesan cheese. Serve immediately.

Advance Preparation: The sauce can be prepared 4 hours in advance and kept covered at room temperature.

2 pounds ripe plum (Roma) tomatoes, peeled, seeded, and coarsely chopped

¼ cup extra-virgin olive oil

1 bunch fresh basil, coarsely chopped

½ cup finely chopped fresh Italian parsley

4 medium garlic cloves, minced

½ pound fresh mozzarella cheese, cut into ¼-inch dice

½ cup freshly grated Parmesan cheese

Salt to taste, plus 1 teaspoon

Freshly ground black pepper

1 pound spaghetti or linguine

Garnish

fresh basil leaves

✳ grilled cheese

Grilled cheese can be more than just the favorite American sandwich. Try wrapping chunks of a good melting cheese, such as provolone, Italian Fontina, or Monterey Jack, in rinsed jarred grape leaves, and then skewer them for the barbecue. Grill them until the cheese softens and serve immediately. You can also marinate the cheese in herbs and extra-virgin olive oil before wrapping it. Feta and fresh goat cheeses are also delicious grilled, but because they melt very quickly, they require careful attention.

with summer vegetables
spicycapellini

SERVES 4–6

Capellini, a thin, delicate pasta also known as angel hair, goes nicely with this colorful variety of fresh summer vegetables. The red pepper flakes add a biting hotness to the sauce, and if you've never tried aged California goat cheese as a variation on Parmesan cheese, you'll be pleasantly surprised. Add a small amount of Summer Vinaigrette (page 182) to any leftovers for a delicious pasta salad. Serve the pasta with a simple green salad and Herbed Garlic Cheese Bread (page 41) for a light Sunday dinner.

1. In a very deep, large skillet over medium-high heat, warm 1 tablespoon of the olive oil. Add the zucchini and sauté, stirring occasionally, until crisp-tender, about 3 minutes. Transfer to a bowl.

2. Heat the remaining olive oil in the same skillet over medium heat. Add the shallots and sauté until softened, 2 to 3 minutes. Add the garlic and cook for another minute. Add the tomatoes and cook, stirring, until softened, 2 to 3 minutes. Add the chicken stock, 2 tablespoons of the basil, salt to taste, and red pepper flakes. Bring to a simmer and let cook until slightly reduced and thickened, 3 to 4 minutes longer.

3. Add the corn and olives and cook for 1 minute. Return the zucchini to the sauce and cook until just heated through. Add the remaining 2 tablespoons basil and stir to combine. Taste for seasoning.

4. Bring a large pot of water to a boil. Add the 1 teaspoon salt and the pasta, stir well, and boil until al dente, 4 to 6 minutes. Drain well and place in a large serving bowl.

5. Pour three-fourths of the vegetable sauce over the pasta. Garnish with a few tablespoons of the cheese, then toss together the pasta and the sauce until the vegetables are evenly distributed. Serve the pasta in soup plates, topping each portion with an extra spoonful of the remaining sauce. Sprinkle the remaining Parmesan cheese on top. Serve immediately.

Advance Preparation: The sauce may be prepared 4 hours in advance through step 2 and kept covered at room temperature.

¼ cup extra-virgin olive oil

1 pound zucchini (4 medium), or a mixture of yellow and green zucchini

3 medium shallots, finely chopped

3 medium garlic cloves, minced

6 large tomatoes (about 3 pounds), peeled, seeded, and finely chopped

1 cup chicken stock

¼ cup finely chopped fresh basil

salt to taste, plus 1 teaspoon

Freshly ground black pepper

¼ teaspoon red pepper flakes, or to taste

1 cup corn kernels (from about 2 medium ears)

½ cup pitted, chopped Kalamata olives

1 pound capellini

Garnish

½ cup freshly grated Parmesan or aged California goat cheese

ravioli nudi

This recipe is perfect for those occasions when you want the taste of pasta without the bulk. Where's the pasta? Not in this dish. Poached spinach-ricotta balls are the "nude" ravioli, sauced with sweet-peppers and tomatoes. This recipe was inspired by one from Giuliano Bugialli, the noted Italian culinary historian and teacher. You can serve it as a first course or as a side dish with simple grilled foods. It also makes a light vegetarian luncheon dish when accompanied by Garden Salad with Goat Cheese–Thyme Dressing (page 80).

1. In a large skillet over medium heat, pour in water to a depth of ½ inch. Add the spinach, cover, and steam for 3 to 5 minutes. Drain, rinse the spinach in cold water until cool, then place in a dry dish towel and squeeze out all the excess liquid. (This is important because too much liquid will prevent the ravioli from holding together.)

2. With a large, sharp knife, finely chop the spinach and place in a medium bowl.

3. Add the ricotta, egg yolks, Parmesan cheese, nutmeg, ½ teaspoon of the salt, and the pepper. Mix together until completely blended.

4. Fill a large, deep sauté pan or Dutch oven three-fourths full of water. Add the remaining 1 teaspoon salt and bring to a boil over high heat.

5. Spread the flour on a baking sheet. With your hands, form the spinach mixture into balls the size of large walnuts. As each ball is formed, roll it in the flour until evenly coated, then set aside on a plate.

6. To test the cooking time for the ravioli, drop a ball into the boiling water. It should come to the surface in about 2 minutes. Break it open to see if it is done in the center. If it is not done, you will need to increase the cooking time; if it is overdone, you will need to reduce it.

7. Continue cooking the ravioli, adding about 6 at a time to the boiling water and cooking until done. Immediately transfer them to shallow pasta bowls.

8. Spoon the sauce over the ravioli and serve immediately. Pass the Parmesan cheese at the table.

Advance Preparation: The ravioli may be prepared 4 hours in advance through step 3 and refrigerated.

2½ pounds spinach (about 4 bunches), rinsed

1 pound (2 cups) ricotta cheese

4 egg yolks

1½ cups freshly grated Parmesan cheese

¼ teaspoon nutmeg, preferably freshly grated

1½ teaspoons salt

¼ teaspoon freshly ground black pepper

1 cup all-purpose flour

2 cups Red Pepper–Tomato Sauce (page 190), heated

Garnish

½ cup freshly grated Parmesan cheese

parslied**couscous**

SERVES 4

Easy, attractive, delicious, and healthy—what more could you want? This dish is also perfect for last-minute entertaining because it takes just a short time to prepare and calls for ingredients that are usually on hand. Serve as an accompaniment to Grilled Swordfish with Herbed Green Sauce (page 96) or Sautéed Chicken with Tomato-Leek Sauce (page 114). Entrées with spicy sauces are complemented nicely by this simple side dish.

1. In a medium saucepan over medium-high heat, bring 1½ cups of the water to a simmer. Add the carrots, cover, and cook for 2 minutes. Add the zucchini, re-cover, and cook for another 2 minutes. Drain the vegetables in a colander and set aside.
2. In the same saucepan over medium heat, bring the remaining 1½ cups water to a boil. Add the couscous and the butter, cover, and remove from the heat. Let stand for 5 minutes.
3. Add the carrots, zucchini, parsley, and salt and pepper to taste to the couscous and toss to combine. Taste for seasoning.
4. Spoon into a serving dish and serve immediately.

Advance Preparation: This may be prepared up to 2 hours in advance and kept covered at room temperature. Reheat it carefully in the top of a double boiler above boiling water for 10 minutes.

3 cups water

2 medium carrots, peeled and cut into ⅛-inch pieces

2 medium zucchini, cut into ⅛-inch pieces

1 cup quick-cooking couscous

2 tablespoons unsalted butter

2 tablespoons finely chopped fresh Italian parsley

salt and freshly ground black pepper

orzo

SERVES 4

Orzo is a tiny, almond-shaped pasta that looks a lot like rice. This creamy dish should be made only moments before serving, so it's a good idea to prepare it for a small informal dinner party. The goat cheese adds a dimension of pungent flavor beyond the more predictable Parmesan or pecorino romano. Serve this as a first course or as a side dish to Grilled Chicken with Sun-Dried-Tomato Marinade (page 115).

1. Preheat the oven to 350°F. Toast the pine nuts until lightly browned, 5 to 7 minutes. Set aside.

2. Place the zucchini in a clean dish towel and squeeze out as much juice as possible.

3. In a medium skillet over medium heat, melt the butter with the olive oil. Add the shallot and sauté until softened, about 3 minutes. Add the zucchini and continue to sauté until beginning to soften, about 3 minutes. Add the mushrooms and sauté for 2 to 3 minutes more. Keep warm.

4. Bring a large pot of water with the salt to a boil. Add the orzo, stir well, and boil until al dente, 8 to 10 minutes. Drain.

5. Meanwhile, in a small saucepan over low heat, combine the cream and goat cheese and stir until the cheese is softened.

6. In a serving bowl, combine the sautéed vegetables, orzo, warmed goat cheese, Parmesan cheese, and basil. Carefully stir in the pine nuts. Add the salt and pepper and taste for seasoning. Toss well and serve immediately.

Advance Preparation: The vegetables may be prepared 4 hours in advance through step 3 and kept covered at room temperature. Reheat gently.

3 tablespoons pine nuts

2 medium green zucchini, cut into ¼-inch dice

2 medium yellow zucchini or crookneck squashes, cut into ¼-inch dice

2 tablespoons unsalted butter

1 tablespoon olive oil

1 large shallot, finely chopped

½ pound fresh mushrooms, cut into ¼-inch dice

1 teaspoon salt

1 cup orzo

2 tablespoons whipping cream

¼ pound fresh goat cheese

¼ cup freshly grated Parmesan cheese

2 tablespoons finely chopped fresh basil

salt and freshly ground black pepper

pizza**dough**

MAKES TWO
9-INCH PIZZA
CRUSTS

You can usually buy pizza dough from a good pizzeria—an ideal solution for the summer cook. Purists will want to make their own, however, and this food processor method is very easy.

1. In a small bowl, sprinkle the dry yeast or crumble the fresh yeast over ¼ cup of the lukewarm water. Let stand for 10 minutes until creamy on top, then stir to dissolve the yeast.
2. In a food processor, combine the flour and salt and process briefly to mix. Add the remaining ¾ cup water and the olive oil to the yeast mixture. With the motor running, gradually pour in the yeast-liquid mixture. If the dough is too dry to hold together, add 1 tablespoon water and process again. Process for 1 minute to knead the dough.
3. Transfer the dough to a clean bowl and sprinkle with a little flour. Cover the bowl with a damp dish towel and let the dough rise in a warm place until doubled in volume, about 1 hour.
4. Punch down the dough and knead again briefly on a floured surface until smooth. Return to the bowl and re-cover.
5. Let the dough rise until doubled in volume, 30 to 45 minutes.
6. Shape according to directions in individual recipes.

Advance Preparation: The dough may be prepared up to 8 hours ahead through step 4 and refrigerated. To continue, remove from the refrigerator and let rise for 20 to 30 minutes, then shape according to individual recipes.

2 envelopes (¼ ounce each) active dry yeast, or 2 cakes (¾ ounce each) fresh yeast

1 cup lukewarm water

3 cups all-purpose flour

1½ teaspoons salt

2 tablespoons olive oil

barbecued pizza
with leeks, mozzarella, tomatoes, and pancetta

MAKES 2
PIZZAS;
SERVES 2–4
AS A MAIN
COURSE OR
6–8 AS AN
APPETIZER

I've often thought that grilled pizza would be the ultimate summer recipe. One day I was cooking at the Parkway Grill in Pasadena, California, and I told chef Hugo Molina about my idea. Since the Parkway is renowned for its pizza, Hugo couldn't wait to try it. The result was a wonderful surprise. The pizza had a delightful smoky taste, the grill-marked crust was crispy, and the toppings were perfectly cooked. ✳ *I was so enthusiastic I experimented with an assortment of pizzas on my home grill that night. A grill with a lid works best. This combination is my favorite. If pancetta, the dry-cured Italian bacon, isn't available, substitute thickly sliced bacon.*

1. To make the topping, slice the tomatoes crosswise. Place the slices in a colander and let drain for 30 minutes to remove any excess liquid.

2. In a deep sauté pan over low heat, warm the olive oil. Add the leeks and mix thoroughly. Cover and cook over very low heat, stirring often, until tender, 15 to 20 minutes. If any liquid remains in the pan, uncover and continue cooking, stirring, until it evaporates. Season with the salt and pepper.

3. In a medium skillet, cook the pancetta over medium-low heat until crisp and slightly brown, about 7 minutes. Using a slotted spoon, transfer to paper towels to drain.

4. Place the tomatoes, pancetta, leeks, and mozzarella in separate small bowls. Reserve.

5. When ready to barbecue, prepare the barbecue for medium-high-heat grilling. (If your barbecue has no cover, improvise one out of aluminum foil or use a large rounded lid.)

6. Oil 2 round baking sheets or pizza pans. Knead the dough again briefly and divide it in half. Put each on a baking sheet or pan. With oiled hands, pat each piece of dough into a 9-inch round. You may also roll out the dough on a floured surface, using a rolling pin, and transfer the rounds to the baking sheets.

7. Brush the tops of the pizzas with 2 tablespoons of the olive oil. Using a large spatula, transfer the pizzas to the center of the grill and cook until the dough begins to puff and there are grill marks on the bottom, about 2 minutes.

Topping

½ pound ripe plum (Roma) tomatoes

3 tablespoons olive oil

3 medium leeks, white and light
    green parts, thinly sliced

salt and freshly ground black pepper

½ pound pancetta, cut into
    1-inch pieces

1½ cups shredded mozzarella
    cheese

Pizza Dough (page 73)

¼ cup olive oil

¼ cup finely chopped fresh basil

recipe continues ▶

8. Using the large spatula, turn the pizza crusts over and move them to the coolest part of the grill. Brush the grilled tops of the crusts with the remaining 2 tablespoons oil. Divide the leek mixture between the 2 crusts, spreading it evenly. Sprinkle ¾ cup of the mozzarella cheese over each crust. Divide and arrange the pancetta pieces on top, then divide and overlap the tomato slices in an attractive pattern. Sprinkle with the basil.

9. Move the pizzas into the center of the grill, cover, and grill for 3 minutes. Check the pizzas and rotate them. Re-cover and cook for 2 to 3 minutes more. Watch carefully so that they do not burn on the bottom. The cheese should be completely melted. (If you want them hotter on top, you can place them under a preheated broiler for a minute or two.) They should be slightly charred.

10. Place on platters and cut into wedges with a pizza wheel. Serve immediately.

☀ pizza toppings

Thinking up toppings for pizza is fun, and the possibilities are almost countless. I tend to prefer simple combinations, but every now and then I want one with the "works," like the Mexican-style pizza. Here are some of my favorites:

Plum (Roma) tomato, mozzarella cheese, and fresh basil

Pesto sauce, Italian Fontina cheese, and cooked shrimp

Goat cheese, arugula, and cooked chicken

Goat cheese and black olives

Grilled eggplant, tomato, Parmesan cheese, and thyme

Mexican-style: Sautéed onion, roasted chilies, tomatoes,
  Cheddar cheese, and fresh cilantro, topped with avocado and sour cream

Roasted garlic, sun-dried tomatoes, and goat cheese

Mascarpone cheese, smoked salmon, and caviar

Yellow and red cherry tomatoes, red onion, cooked and sliced sweet and
  hot Italian sausage, and Parmesan cheese

salads

three-lettuce salad
with tomato-tarragon dressing

SERVES 4–6

Crisp and colorful, this first course salad is simple enough to go with a number of different entrées. While Belgian endive used to be thought of as a winter vegetable, it is now available year-round. Pureed tomatoes add extra body to the tarragon vinaigrette. For a casual meal, serve the salad before a steaming bowl of Corn Chowder with Red Peppers (page 55) and hot sourdough French rolls. For dessert follow with Lattice Crust Pie with Rhubarb, Peaches, Strawberries, and Plums (page 165).

1. To make the dressing, finely chop the shallot and garlic in a food processor. With the motor running, add the tomatoes and process until pureed. Add the mustard, tarragon, and vinegar and process until well blended.

2. With the motor running, slowly add the olive oil, processing until completely blended. Add the cream and season with salt and pepper. Process just until combined. Taste for seasoning.

3. To make the salad, arrange the butter lettuce and radicchio in a shallow salad bowl. Slice 2 endive leaves crosswise into ¼-inch-wide slices and scatter on top of the lettuce. Separate the other endive leaves and arrange along the edge of the bowl.

4. Arrange the cucumber in the center, then surround it with the carrots, creating a colorful circular pattern.

5. When ready to serve, arrange the avocado slices around the outside edge. Pour the dressing over and serve.

Advance Preparation: This may be prepared 4 hours in advance through step 4 and refrigerated until serving. The dressing may be prepared 2 days in advance and refrigerated.

Dressing

1 medium shallot

1 medium garlic clove

½ pound tomatoes, peeled, seeded, and chopped

2 teaspoons Dijon mustard

1 tablespoon finely chopped fresh tarragon

3 tablespoons white wine vinegar

½ cup olive oil

1 tablespoon whipping cream

salt and freshly ground black pepper

Salad

1 medium head butter lettuce, torn into bite-size pieces

1 small head radicchio, torn into bite-size pieces

4 medium heads Belgian endive

½ English cucumber, julienned

3 medium carrots, peeled and julienned

1 medium avocado, pitted, peeled, and cut into ¼-inch-thick slices

These splendid salad dressings are not only for salads. You can also use them to dress grilled or steamed vegetables or grilled chicken, fish, or meat—a particularly appealing idea when you want a sauce but don't want to cook.

A successful vinaigrette depends upon excellent ingredients, the correct ratio of oil to vinegar, and the complete emulsification of the two. I prefer a ratio of three parts oil to one part vinegar. I use my food processor to make vinaigrette because it creates an emulsion that will last at least a few hours. If you don't have a food processor, put the ingredients in a small lidded jar and shake vigorously to emulsify. Vinaigrette will keep in the refrigerator for months. Just bring it to room temperature before using and whisk or process to re-emulsify.

An enormous variety of excellent oils and vinegar is available, allowing you to be endlessly creative. Keep on hand extra-virgin olive oil, safflower oil, aged sherry wine vinegar, tarragon vinegar, a quality red wine vinegar, and balsamic vinegar. Avocado oil, Champagne vinegar, and raspberry vinegar make interesting alternatives. The flavors of hazelnut oil and walnut oil are very intense, and the oils should be used sparingly. I recommend using half nut oil and half olive oil. Almost all vinaigrettes should include a minced shallot and a garlic clove. Dijon mustard is another excellent flavor enhancer. Finally, for a milder vinaigrette, I like to add just a touch of cream to smooth out the acid in the vinegar. Here are some other combinations you might try:

Red onion vinaigrette

Tomato-basil vinaigrette

Chervil, dill, or burnet vinaigrette

Tomato-mint vinaigrette

Hazelnut or walnut vinaigrette

Chopped olive vinaigrette

Roasted chile vinaigrette

Red or green sweet pepper vinaigrette

vinaigrettes

garden salad with goat cheese–thyme dressing

The dressing is the unique element of this salad, with the goat cheese and eggs conjuring up a cross between Roquefort and Caesar dressing. The bite of the fresh thyme offsets the creamy richness of the goat cheese. Follow with Grilled Mexican Chicken with Citrus Yogurt Sauce (page 116) and a double recipe of Parslied Couscous with Zucchini and Carrots (page 70).

1. To make the dressing, in a blender or food processor, combine the garlic and vinegar and process to mix well. With the motor running, slowly pour in the olive oil and cooked eggs. Add the goat cheese and process until creamy. Add the thyme and season with salt and pepper. Process briefly, then taste for seasoning.
2. To make the salad, place the butter lettuce on individual salad plates and arrange the vegetables on top in an attractive manner, distributing the cherry tomatoes around the edge. Sprinkle with the goat cheese.
3. To serve, drizzle the dressing over the salad and garnish with the thyme leaves, if you like.

Advance Preparation: This may be prepared 4 hours in advance through step 2 and refrigerated.

Note: You may have extra dressing; cover and refrigerate for up to 4 days.

Dressing

2 medium garlic cloves, minced

6 tablespoons red wine vinegar

1 cup plus 3 tablespoons olive oil

2 eggs, boiled for 3 minutes

2 ounces fresh goat cheese

1½ teaspoons finely chopped fresh thyme

salt and freshly ground black pepper

Salad

2 medium heads butter lettuce, torn into bite-size pieces

1 medium jicama (about ½ pound), peeled and julienned or shredded

2 medium carrots, peeled and julienned or shredded

12 red or yellow cherry tomatoes, or a combination, halved

2 tablespoons crumbled goat cheese

Garnish

Fresh thyme leaves (optional)

One of my favorite summer sandwiches is *pan bagnat,* the Provençal salad sandwich. To make one, split a portion of a baguette or a sourdough sandwich roll vertically so that the bottom is two-thirds of the loaf or roll and the top is only one-third. Scoop out most of the bread from both pieces, leaving thick crusts lined with thin layers of bread. Brush an herbed vinaigrette, such as Summer Vinaigrette (page 182), on the cut sides of the bread and top with any combination of the ingredients listed here. Layer the vegetables on the bottom, then sprinkle them with a little more vinaigrette. Top with the meats and/or cheeses and close the sandwich. The sandwiches are great for picnics because the flavors improve if they are left to mingle for a few hours, but wrap them tightly and keep in a cooler. If they include cheese, they can also be placed in a grill basket and quickly grilled. Grilling will melt the cheese and give the bread a lovely crisp crust.

Roasted red, green, or yellow sweet pepper slices

Tomato slices

Pitted Niçoise olives

Marinated artichoke hearts

Anchovies

Imported ham (or good-quality domestic)

Roasted chicken slices

Watercress, arugula, or basil leaves

Goat, mozzarella, or provolone cheese

Celery slices

Cucumber slices

Capers

pan bagnat

with yellow pepper, jicama, and tomato
greenbeansalad

SERVES 4–6

Full of crunchy, sweet vegetables, this salad is a terrific addition to a barbecue menu. The high ratio of citrus to oil in the lemon-mustard dressing adds tang, making this a snappy side dish. Serve as an accompaniment to Grilled Steaks, California Style (page 129) or with Grilled Marinated Chicken with Dijon Mustard, Tarragon, and Port (page 117).

1. To make the salad, bring a medium saucepan of water to a boil. Immerse the green beans and cook for 7 to 10 minutes, depending on their size. The beans should be slightly crisp. Drain and place in ice water to stop the cooking. When cool, drain well and place in a medium bowl.
2. Add the peppers, jicama, and tomatoes to the green beans.
3. To make the dressing, in a small bowl, combine the mustard, lemon juice, and chives. Whisk to combine, then slowly add the olive oil, whisking until totally emulsified. Season with salt and pepper.
4. Drizzle the dressing over the vegetables and toss thoroughly. Taste for seasoning. Transfer to a serving bowl, cover, and refrigerate until well chilled, at least 1 hour.

Advance Preparation: This may be completely prepared 8 hours in advance and refrigerated until serving.

Salad

1 pound green beans, trimmed

1 yellow sweet pepper, seeded
    and julienned

1 medium jicama (about ½ pound),
    peeled and julienned

15 cherry tomatoes, halved

Dressing

1 teaspoon Dijon mustard

⅓ cup fresh lemon juice

1 teaspoon finely chopped
    fresh chives

⅔ cup olive oil

salt and freshly ground black pepper

colorful coleslaw

You'll love this fresh version of an old standard. The flavor is best if you prepare the salad a few hours ahead of serving or even the night before. Serve with Sweet and Hot Spareribs with Apricot-Plum Sauce (page 130).

1. To make the dressing, combine all the ingredients in small nonaluminum bowl, including salt and pepper to taste, and whisk to blend. Set aside.
2. To make the salad, combine all the ingredients in a large bowl.
3. Toss the salad with enough of the dressing to moisten well. Taste for seasoning.
4. Mound the cabbage mixture in a large, shallow serving bowl. Garnish with the parsley and serve.

Advance Preparation: This may be completely prepared 1 day in advance and refrigerated. Taste for seasoning before serving.

Dressing

1 cup plus 2 tablespoons
    mayonnaise

6 tablespoons cider vinegar

1 tablespoon fresh lemon juice

2 to 3 tablespoons sugar, to taste

salt and freshly ground white pepper

Salad

1 medium green cabbage,
    finely shredded

4 medium carrots, peeled and
    finely shredded

1 medium bunch radishes,
    finely shredded

1 small Granny Smith or pippin
    apple, peeled, cored,
    and shredded

3 tablespoons finely chopped
    fresh parsley

1 tablespoon finely chopped fresh dill

2 tablespoons finely chopped
    red onion

Garnish

2 tablespoons finely chopped
    fresh parsley

crackedwheat–vegetablesalad

This is a variation on tabbouleh, the Middle Eastern cracked-wheat salad made with lots of olive oil, lemon, mint, tomato, and parsley. In this version, cilantro replaces parsley and instead of tomatoes we have raw corn, chopped cucumber, and radishes. Summer corn is so sweet and tender that you don't need to cook it for this recipe. Be sure to buy medium cracked wheat. If you want to substitute bulgur wheat for cracked wheat, you will need to soak it in hot water for only 20 to 30 minutes.

1. To make the salad, place the cracked wheat in a medium bowl, pour the boiling water over it, and let stand until the wheat absorbs the water. This should take about 1 hour.
2. Pour the wheat into a colander to drain off any excess water. Transfer to a kitchen towel and wring out any additional moisture. Place in a medium bowl.
3. Add the red onion, cucumber, radishes, carrots, and corn. Mix with a two-pronged fork to keep the wheat fluffy. Add the parsley, chives, and cilantro.
4. To make the dressing, in a medium bowl, whisk together all the ingredients until well blended.
5. Pour the dressing over the wheat mixture and toss with two forks. Taste for seasoning. Place in a serving bowl, garnish with the cilantro leaves, and serve.

Advance Preparation: This may be prepared 8 hours ahead and refrigerated.

Salad

1½ cups medium cracked wheat

2½ cups boiling water

½ cup finely chopped red onion

½ cup finely diced English cucumber

¾ cup finely diced radishes

¾ cup peeled and finely diced carrots

¾ cup corn kernels (from about 1
    large ear)

2 tablespoons finely chopped
    fresh parsley

2 tablespoons finely chopped
    fresh chives

3 tablespoons finely chopped
    fresh cilantro

Dressing

½ cup Summer Vinaigrette (page 182)

2 tablespoons fresh lemon juice

salt and freshly ground black pepper

Garnish

fresh cilantro leaves

with caviar-dill mayonnaise
coldlobstersalad

SERVES 4

In this elegant salad, sweet lobster is dressed with a lemony mayonnaise and decorated with sprigs of dill and bright orange salmon caviar. Serve it for a truly special occasion, for it's not only extravagant but also memorably delicious. Start with Golden Summer Soup (page 44) and accompany the salad with Toasted Pita with Parmesan (page 42). For dessert serve Frozen Peaches and Cream (page 178) or Poached Peaches in White Zinfandel with Raspberry Sauce (page 156).

 SERVE WITH CHAMPAGNE.

1. Split the lobsters in half. With a small knife, carefully separate the meat from the shells. Try to keep the shells intact.
2. Cut the lobster meat into 1-inch pieces and place in a medium bowl.
3. To make the dressing, in a small bowl, combine the mayonnaise, lemon juice, dill, and salt and pepper to taste and mix to combine. Gently stir in the caviar, being careful not to mash it. Taste for seasoning.
4. Pour just enough dressing over the lobster to moisten it well and then toss to coat evenly. Cover the lobster and the remaining dressing and refrigerate until ready to serve.
5. Just before serving, mound one-fourth of the lobster mixture in each lobster shell. Spoon a dollop of the remaining dressing on top, and garnish with a large spoonful of salmon caviar and a dill sprig. Serve immediately.

Advance Preparation: This may be prepared up to 2 hours in advance through step 4 and refrigerated. Keep the lobster shells well wrapped in the refrigerator until ready to assemble the dish.

Variation: This salad may be placed on a bed of mixed greens that have been lightly dressed with Summer Vinaigrette (page 182).

2 lobsters, about 1½ pounds each, boiled or steamed, and chilled

Dressing

⅔ cup mayonnaise

¼ cup fresh lemon juice

3 tablespoons finely chopped fresh dill

salt and freshly ground white pepper

¼ cup salmon caviar

Garnish

2 tablespoons salmon caviar

4 fresh dill sprigs

with celery seed
red**potato**salad

For this salad, the red skins are left on the potatoes for extra color and texture. Celery seed and celery add freshness and crispness, as well as a counterpoint to the tangy chives. This salad is perfect with cold roasted chicken.

1. In a large pot, combine the potatoes with water to cover generously. Bring to a boil and cook until tender but slightly resistant when pierced with a fork, about 30 minutes. Drain and cool, but do not peel. When cool, cut into 1½-inch pieces and place in a medium bowl.
2. To make the dressing, in a small bowl, whisk together the sour cream, mayonnaise, celery, celery seeds, chives, mustard, parsley, and salt and pepper to taste. Mix well.
3. Pour the mixture over the potatoes and toss gently until evenly coated. Taste for seasoning. Cover and refrigerate for 1 to 2 hours.
4. Transfer the salad to a serving bowl and garnish with the parsley and chives. Serve cold.

Advance Preparation: This may be prepared 1 day in advance through step 3 and refrigerated. Taste for seasoning before serving.

3 pounds medium red potatoes

Dressing

¾ cup sour cream

¾ cup mayonnaise

2 celery stalks, finely diced

1 tablespoon celery seeds

2 tablespoons chopped fresh chives

1 teaspoon dry mustard

¼ cup chopped fresh parsley

salt and freshly ground white pepper

Garnish

1 tablespoon chopped fresh parsley

1 tablespoon finely chopped
  fresh chives

chickensalad
with roasted garlic mayonnaise

SERVES 4–6

The Roasted Garlic Mayonnaise (page 186) adds a sweet, mild pungency to this main-course chicken salad. Toasted almonds and crisp broccoli give it extra texture. Begin with Golden Summer Soup (page 44) and serve Toasted Pita with Parmesan (page 42) with the salad. For dessert, offer Summer Fruit Compote (page 158).

 A BIG, OAKY CHARDONNAY WORKS WELL WITH THIS DISH, OR TRY A PINOT NOIR OR A SLIGHTLY CHILLED BEAUJOLAIS.

1. Preheat the oven to 350°F. Toast the almonds until lightly browned, about 5 minutes. Set aside.
2. In a medium skillet with high sides or a large saucepan, bring the chicken stock or water or a combination of chicken stock and water to a simmer. If using water only, add the ½ teaspoon salt.
3. Add the chicken breasts; they should be fully immersed in the liquid. Simmer just until tender, 10 to 12 minutes. Remove from the heat and let the chicken cool in the liquid. Drain, remove and discard the skin, and cut the meat into 1½-inch chunks. Place in a large bowl.
4. Bring a saucepan of water to a boil. Immerse the broccoli florets and simmer until crisp-tender, 7 to 10 minutes. Drain in a colander and run cold water over the top to stop the cooking. Drain well, pat dry, and add to the chicken.
5. Add the scallions and mayonnaise to the chicken and broccoli and toss to mix well.
6. Season with salt and pepper. Cover and refrigerate for at least 2 hours.
7. Just before serving, carefully add all but 2 tablespoons of the toasted almonds, tossing until just mixed. Place in a serving dish and garnish with the red pepper slices and the reserved 2 tablespoons almonds.

Advance Preparation: This may be prepared 1 day in advance through step 6 and refrigerated until ready to serve. Taste for seasoning before serving.

½ cup thinly sliced almonds

about 3 cups chicken stock
and/or water

½ teaspoon salt, if using water, plus
salt to taste

2 pounds boned chicken breasts
(about 2 large whole breasts)

1 pound broccoli, cut into florets

2 tablespoons finely chopped
scallions or fresh chives

1 cup Roasted Garlic Mayonnaise
(page 186)

freshly ground white pepper

Garnish
1 roasted red sweet pepper, thinly
sliced (page 196)

chickensaladniçoise

SERVES 6–8

The classic salade niçoise is made with tuna, but I prefer the lighter taste of chicken. A hearty combination of flavors, colors, and textures, this salad is an excellent main dish for lunch, dinner, or a late-night supper. Start with Goat Cheese and Pesto Torta with Hazelnuts (page 34) and then serve Creamy Gazpacho (page 50). French or Italian country bread goes nicely with the salad, followed by Strawberry Shortcake with Raspberry Custard Sauce (page 161).

 SERVE A BIG, OAKY CHARDONNAY OR A SLIGHTLY CHILLED BEAUJOLAIS.

1. In a medium skillet with high sides or a large saucepan, bring the chicken stock or water or a combination of chicken stock and water to a simmer. If using water only, add the ½ teaspoon salt.

2. Add the chicken breasts; they should be fully immersed in the liquid. Simmer just until tender, 10 to 12 minutes. Remove from the heat and let the chicken cool in the liquid. Drain, remove and discard the skin, and shred the meat by tearing into long, thin pieces. Place in a large bowl.

3. In a large pot, combine the potatoes with water to cover generously. Bring to a boil and cook until tender but slightly resistant when pierced with a fork, 20 to 30 minutes. Drain and let cool. When cool, peel and cut into julienne. Add to the bowl with the chicken.

4. Bring a medium saucepan full of water to a boil. Immerse the green beans and cook until tender but slightly resistant, 5 to 7 minutes. Drain and place in ice water to stop the cooking. When cool, drain well, pat dry, and add to the chicken and potatoes.

5. Add the carrots, red pepper, olives, red onion, capers, chervil or basil, and pepper to taste to the chicken. Toss to combine.

6. To make the dressing, in a small bowl, combine the garlic, mustard, chervil or basil, and lemon juice. Slowly whisk in the olive oil until thoroughly combined. Season with salt and pepper.

7. Add just enough dressing to the salad to moisten it. Toss carefully to combine, making sure not to break up the capers. Taste for seasoning.

about 3 cups chicken stock
    and/or water

½ teaspoon salt, if using water

3 whole chicken breasts, boned

1 pound red-skinned potatoes

½ cup cut-up green beans
    (1½-inch pieces)

2 medium carrots, peeled
    and julienned

1 small red sweet pepper, seeded
    and julienned

½ cup Niçoise olives

1 small red onion, thinly sliced and
    then cut into 1½-inch pieces

2 tablespoons capers, rinsed
    and drained

2 tablespoons finely chopped fresh
    chervil or basil

freshly ground black pepper

recipe continues ▶

8. Mound the salad high in a large, shallow bowl. Alternate the egg wedges and tomato wedges around the outside edge. Garnish with chervil sprigs or basil leaves and serve. Pass the remaining dressing at the table.

Advance Preparation: This salad may be prepared through step 6 up to 6 hours ahead. Refrigerate the salad with the potatoes at the bottom of the bowl. The dressing may be prepared and kept covered at room temperature. The salad may be made completely ahead, including the garnish, up to 2 hours before serving and refrigerated.

✺ cooking a lobster

If your lobster-cooking experience matches the lobster scene in *Annie Hall,* take heart. It's really not that difficult.

1. Choose the feistiest lobsters you can find. Active lobsters are fresher and sweeter.
2. Fill a 16-quart pot two-thirds full of water. If you have seawater at hand, use it instead of fresh water. Add some lemon slices, lemon juice, and peppercorns and bring to a rapid boil. Place the live lobsters in the pot, cover, and cook for about 10 minutes (for 2-pound lobsters). They will have turned red.
3. Using tongs, lift out the lobsters and let cool slightly. With poultry shears, cut the shells in half lengthwise, dividing the lobsters in two. Remove the stomach sacs and discard.
4. Serve the lobsters hot with an herbed garlic butter or chilled with chervil or dill vinaigrette.

Dressing

2 medium garlic cloves, minced

2 teaspoons Dijon mustard

2 tablespoons finely chopped fresh
    chervil or basil

2/3 cup fresh lemon juice

1 cup extra-virgin olive oil

salt and freshly ground black pepper

Garnish

3 hard-cooked eggs, quartered

2 small tomatoes, each cut into
    6 wedges

fresh chervil sprigs or basil leaves
    and flowers

main courses: seafood, poultry, and meats

grilledswordfish

SERVES 6

The green sauce that accompanies this fish derives its earthy and piquant flavor from capers and corni-chons. Make sure to use a fruity extra-virgin olive oil for maximum flavor. This sauce is also wonderful with other grilled fish or chicken pieces. Serve with Parslied Couscous with Zucchini and Carrots (page 70).

 A RICH, OAK-AGED SAUVIGNON BLANC (FUMÉ BLANC IS THE SAME WINE) WORKS WELL WITH THIS DISH.

1. To make the marinade, in a small bowl, stir together the garlic, shallots, lemon juice, and lemon zest. Add the olive oil and stir until blended. Season with salt and pepper.

2. Arrange the swordfish steaks in a large, shallow non aluminum dish. Pour the marinade over the fish, coating evenly. Cover and refrigerate for 2 to 4 hours.

3. Prepare the barbecue for medium heat grilling.

4. To make the sauce, in a medium bowl, whisk together the parsley, shallot, garlic, lemon zest, capers, gherkins, lemon juice, and salt and pepper to taste until combined. Pour in the oil in a steady stream, whisking until well incorporated. (You can also do this in a food processor using a pulsing action. Be careful not to puree the mixture.) Taste for seasoning.

5. Remove the fish from marinade. Grill the fish about 3 inches from the fire, turning once, for 5 to 6 minutes on each side for medium rare, or to desired doneness.

6. Transfer the swordfish to a serving platter and spoon the herbed green sauce on top. Serve immediately.

Advance Preparation: The sauce may be prepared 4 hours ahead and kept covered at room temperature.

Marinade

2 medium garlic cloves, minced

2 medium shallots, finely chopped

6 tablespoons fresh lemon juice

1½ teaspoons minced lemon zest

¼ cup olive oil

salt and freshly ground black pepper

6 swordfish steaks, ⅓ to
    ½ pound each

Sauce

½ cup finely chopped fresh parsley

1 medium shallot, finely chopped

1 medium garlic clove, minced

1 teaspoon finely chopped
    lemon zest

1 tablespoon capers, finely chopped

3 tablespoons finely chopped fresh
    sour gherkins (cornichons)

3 tablespoons fresh lemon juice

salt and freshly ground black pepper

½ cup fruity extra-virgin olive oil

scallops brochette
with spicy caribbean salsa

SERVES 4–6

Warm tropical breezes will come to mind every time you serve this intensely flavorful salsa with grilled scallops. Sea or ocean scallops are larger than bay scallops and work best for this recipe. Cook the scallops until golden brown on the outside and still moist on the inside. The salsa is a perfect companion to other grilled fish, such as halibut, sea bass, whitefish, or shrimp. Serve the brochettes with Sautéed Zucchini and Arugula (page 137) and Cracked Wheat–Vegetable Salad (page 86).

 SERVE AN OFF-DRY GEWÜRZTRAMINER, A SAUVIGNON BLANC THAT IS ON THE LEMONY SIDE, OR BEER.

1. To make the salsa, in a medium skillet over medium heat, warm 2 tablespoons of the olive oil. Add the shallots and sauté until softened, about 3 minutes. Remove from the heat and spoon into a medium bowl. Add all the remaining salsa ingredients, including salt and pepper to taste, and mix well. Taste for seasoning. Cover and refrigerate until 1 hour before serving, then remove from the refrigerator to warm to room temperature.

2. If using bamboo skewers, soak 4 to 6 skewers in cold water for at least 30 minutes to prevent burning during grilling.

3. To make the marinade, in a small bowl, whisk together all of the ingredients.

4. Thread the scallops onto the skewers and lay in a shallow nonaluminum dish. Pour the marinade over the scallops, coating evenly, and marinate at room temperature for 30 minutes.

5. Prepare the barbecue for medium-high-heat grilling. Grill the scallops 3 inches from the fire, turning once, until just opaque throughout, 3 to 4 minutes on each side.

6. Place the brochettes on a serving platter and garnish with the salsa. Serve immediately.

Advance Preparation: The salsa may be prepared 1 day in advance and refrigerated. Remove from the refrigerator 1 hour before serving.

Note: When working with chilies, always wear rubber gloves. Wash the cutting surface and knife immediately afterward.

Salsa

¼ cup olive oil

5 large shallots, finely chopped

2 medium garlic cloves, minced

1 medium bunch fresh chives, finely chopped

2 medium serrano chilies, seeded and finely chopped (see note)

salt and freshly ground black pepper

¼ cup fresh lime juice

Marinade

2 tablespoons finely chopped fresh chives

1 medium garlic clove, minced

2 tablespoons fresh lime juice

1 tablespoon olive oil

salt and freshly ground black pepper

2 pounds sea scallops

roasted sea bass

with herbs

SERVES 4

This simple dish is prepared at Antoine's, the elegant restaurant in the Meridien Hotel in Newport Beach, California. I have made a lighter version, however, substituting olive oil for the melted butter. If you are lucky enough to have your own herb garden, use your favorite combination of just-picked herbs to mix into the bread-crumb coating. Serve with Broiled Tomatoes Glazed with Mustard-Herb Mayonnaise (page 140) and Crushed Strawberry Ice Cream (page 176) for dessert.

 A CRISP, STEELY NORTH COAST SAUVIGNON BLANC IS IDEAL WITH THIS WELL-HERBED DISH.

½ cup fresh bread crumbs

¼ cup minced fresh parsley

2 tablespoons minced fresh chives

1 tablespoon minced fresh thyme

2 tablespoons minced fresh basil

salt and freshly ground white pepper

4 center-cut pieces sea bass,
    each ½ pound and about
      1½ inches thick

2 tablespoons olive oil

1. Preheat the oven to 350°F.
2. In a small bowl, stir together the bread crumbs, herbs, and salt and pepper to taste.
3. Place the fish pieces on waxed paper. With your hands, generously rub the oil on both sides of the fish. Sprinkle the bread crumb–herb mixture evenly on the fish, then pat it so that it adheres.
4. Place the fish on a cake rack in a roasting pan. Roast until the fish just flakes, 10 to 15 minutes. To crisp the top, turn the oven to broil and place the fish under the broiler for about 2 minutes.
5. Transfer to a serving platter and serve immediately.

Advance Preparation: This may be prepared 4 hours in advance through step 3 (except for preheating the oven) and refrigerated.

fresh herbs

Although fresh herbs are plentiful in the summer months, there may be those times when you just don't have them on hand. The rule of thumb for substituting dried herbs for fresh is one part dried to three parts fresh. When using fresh herbs, always remove the leaves from the stems and chop only the leaves. Some leaves, like basil and tarragon, should be chopped—or torn—just before serving, as they darken quickly once they are cut.

grilled**halibut**
in lemon-mustard-tarragon marinade

SERVES 6

Fresh tarragon is plentiful late in the spring and into the summer. It is so much more flavorful than its dry counterpart that I try to use it as much as possible while it is in season. Be sure you use French tarragon and not the tasteless, grassy Russian tarragon. The citrus and tarragon give the halibut a zesty flavor that belies its low calorie count. If you want to cut calories even further, cut the olive oil in half or omit it altogether. Serve with herbed rice and steamed zucchini and carrots for a light summer dinner.

 A SPICY, CRISP SAUVIGNON BLANC PROVIDES AN EXCELLENT FOIL FOR THIS DISH.

1. To make the marinade, in a small bowl, whisk together the lemon juice, lemon zest, mustard, tarragon, and chives or scallions. Slowly whisk in the olive oil until well blended. Season with salt and pepper.
2. Arrange the fish pieces in a large, shallow nonaluminum dish. Pour the marinade over the fish, coating evenly. Cover and refrigerate for 30 minutes to 2 hours.
3. Prepare the barbecue for medium-heat grilling.
4. Remove the fish from the marinade. Grill the fish about 3 inches from the fire, turning once, for 5 to 7 minutes on each side, or to desired doneness.
5. Transfer the fish to a platter and garnish with the lemon slices and tarragon. Serve immediately.

Advance Preparation: This may be prepared 2 hours in advance through step 2 and refrigerated.

Marinade

½ cup fresh lemon juice

1 tablespoon minced lemon zest

¼ cup Dijon mustard

3 tablespoons finely chopped
    fresh tarragon

2 tablespoons finely chopped fresh
    chives or scallions

¼ cup olive oil

salt and freshly ground black pepper

6 halibut steaks or fillets,
    ½ pound each

Garnish

lemon slices

fresh tarragon sprigs

wholepoachedsalmon
with pesto-cucumber sauce

SERVES 8

As soon as summer arrives, my phone starts ringing with questions about how I poach a whole salmon. Here's the answer: the key is to cook the fish 10 minutes for each inch of thickness, then to let the salmon cool in its stock for at least 6 hours. This method keeps the fish moist and extremely flavorful. ✳ *Sour cream, mayonnaise, and dill are traditional ingredients to sauce the salmon, but I like the addition of crunchy cucumber and the essence of fresh basil and pine nuts to the traditional sour cream mayonnaise. Serve the salmon for a buffet dinner or luncheon, accompanied with Chilled Asparagus with Red Pepper Vinaigrette (page 144), Cracked Wheat–Vegetable Salad (page 86), and Green Bean Salad with Yellow Pepper, Jicama, and Tomato (page 83).*

 A RICH CHARDONNAY IS NEEDED HERE TO BALANCE THE RICHNESS OF THE SALMON AND ITS CREAMY SAUCE.

1. To make the sauce, in a small bowl, whisk together all the ingredients, including salt and pepper to taste, mixing well. Cover and refrigerate until serving.

2. It is best to use a fish poacher for this recipe. If you do not have one, you can use a large, deep roasting pan with a round metal rack (one that you would use for cooling cakes and cookies) placed in the middle. Wrap the salmon in a triple thickness of cheesecloth, leaving extra cheesecloth to tie at both ends. Use string or plastic twist-ties to secure the ends.

3. Pour the fish stock or water into the poacher or roasting pan. Place the rack in the pan and then lay the salmon on top. Add more fish stock or water to cover, if needed.

4. Place the poacher on two burners over medium heat. Bring the liquid to a rapid simmer and then reduce to a very slow simmer. (If too high, the salmon will fall apart.) Cook for 20 to 30 minutes, depending on the thickness of the fish (10 minutes per inch measured at the thickest part). When done, remove the pan from the heat and let the salmon cool in the liquid for at least 6 hours.

5. Using 2 spatulas, lift the salmon from the liquid and place on a platter. Carefully remove the cheesecloth.

Sauce
¾ cup sour cream

½ cup mayonnaise

¼ cup Spinach Pesto without
    cheese (page 192)

½ cup coarsely chopped
    English cucumber

salt and freshly ground white pepper

1 whole or half salmon, cleaned and
    head removed

about 2 quarts fish stock or water

Garnish
cucumber slices

watercress sprigs

cherry tomatoes

recipe continues ▶

6. Pour off any collected liquid. Remove the skin by pulling it off; it should peel away easily. Use a sharp knife to remove any gray flesh. The salmon should be completely pink. Remove any bones you see with a small pair of pliers. Cover with foil and refrigerate.

7. When ready to serve, decorate the salmon with the cucumbers, watercress sprigs, and cherry tomatoes. Serve the sauce on the side.

Advance Preparation: The salmon and the sauce may be prepared 1 day in advance and refrigerated.

Note: You can also cut the uncooked whole salmon in half lengthwise and poach the halves in separate pieces of cheesecloth. This will give you 2 separate platters, which works out well for a buffet.

 beer

Americans love beer and there is no better time to enjoy a refreshing brew than in warm weather. Beer is usually recognized as the best choice with spicy foods, but it can actually be a suitable companion to just about any dish except dessert.

Lager, a pale, golden brew popular worldwide, is a smooth, crisp beverage that marries particularly well with food. Ale, which is stronger and has more of a bitter aftertaste, should be limited to strong-flavored, hearty foods.

Good beers are produced in virtually every country in the world. Although there is basically no difference in how they are made, beers of certain national origin seem to best complement foods of their own ethnicity. Japanese beer pairs perfectly with sushi, and no beer is better with *mole poblano* than a Mexican beer.

Beer, like wine, can be overchilled. Any beverage that is too cold will stun the tastebuds and cut down on the enjoyment of not only the drink, but also the food that goes with it. Keep the glasses chilled and the beer cool (50°F), not cold.

sweetandspicygrilledsalmon

SERVES 4

Brown sugar, cilantro, and ginger are added here for a sweet and spicy Asian-style sauce. Basting can lend as much flavor to fish as marinating, so remember to brush on the sauce every few minutes. Serve with your favorite grilled vegetable and simple steamed rice. Begin with Minted Chinese Snow Pea Soup (page 46) and finish with a fresh fruit platter and Toasted Almond Cookies with Lemon and Port (page 174).

 SALMON IS RICH AND OILY AND REQUIRES A FAIRLY SUBSTANTIAL WINE TO BALANCE IT. A BARREL-FERMENTED CHARDONNAY IS INDICATED HERE.

1. Prepare the barbecue for medium-heat grilling.
2. In a small saucepan over medium heat, melt the butter. Add the shallots and sauté until softened, about 3 minutes.
3. Add the lemon juice, brown sugar, cayenne pepper, ginger, vinegar, and soy sauce and stir until well combined. Remove from the heat and mix in the cilantro.
4. Baste the salmon liberally on both sides with the sauce.
5. Grill the salmon about 3 inches from the fire, turning once and basting frequently with the sauce, 7 to 10 minutes on each side. The timing will depend on the thickness and size of the salmon pieces.
6. Transfer the salmon to a platter or individual plates and garnish with the lemon slices and parsley. Serve immediately. Pass the remaining sauce at the table.

Advance Preparation: The sauce may be prepared 8 hours in advance and kept covered at room temperature. Reheat the sauce before basting the salmon.

Sauce

1 tablespoon unsalted butter

2 medium shallots, finely chopped

¼ cup fresh lemon juice

4 teaspoons brown sugar

¼ teaspoon cayenne pepper

1 tablespoon finely chopped
   fresh ginger

¼ cup red wine vinegar

2 tablespoons soy sauce

2 tablespoons finely chopped
   fresh cilantro

2 pounds salmon fillets or 4 salmon
   steaks, ½ pound each

Garnish

lemon slices

fresh parsley sprigs

tequila-lime grilled shrimp

SERVES 4–6

This is a great party dish when accompanied with Cuban Black Beans (page 143) and Tomato-Papaya-Mint Salsa (page 193). Add a simple vegetable rice to round out the menu. Begin with frosty margaritas and Guacamole Salsa (page 30) with crisp tortilla chips.

 POUR A CRISP SAUVIGNON BLANC OR FRENCH CHABLIS.

2 pounds large shrimp in the shell

Marinade

¼ cup fresh lime juice

¼ cup tequila

2 medium garlic cloves, minced

2 medium shallots, finely chopped

2 teaspoons ground cumin

salt and freshly ground black pepper

½ cup olive oil

Garnish

lime slices

1 bunch watercress

1. If using bamboo skewers, soak them in cold water for at least 30 minutes to prevent burning during grilling.
2. Thread the shrimp onto the skewers (3 or 4 to each skewer). Lay in a single layer in a shallow nonaluminum dish.
3. To prepare the marinade, whisk together the lime juice, tequila, garlic, shallots, cumin, and salt and pepper to taste. Slowly add the olive oil, whisking until combined. Taste for seasoning.
4. Pour over the shrimp and let marinate for at least 30 minutes or as long as 4 hours in the refrigerator.
5. Prepare the barbecue for medium-heat grilling.
6. Grill the shrimp about 3 inches from the fire, turning once, until cooked through, about 4 minutes on each side. Transfer to a platter and slip the shrimp off the skewers.
7. Garnish with lime slices and watercress. Serve immediately.

Advance Preparation: This may be prepared 4 hours in advance through step 4 and refrigerated.

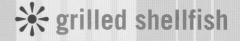

☀ grilled shellfish

If you're in the mood for something light and delicious, grilled shellfish is the answer. Scrub clams, mussels, and oysters under running water, removing any beards from the mussels. Prepare the barbecue for medium-high-heat grilling. Place the shellfish on the grill, cover, and barbecue until they begin to open, 3 to 5 minutes. Serve them in a deep bowl with wedges of lime. They are also great accompanied with Tomatillo Sauce (page 189) or Tomato Basil Sauce (page 187).

with lemon butter
soft-shell crab

SERVES 2
AS A MAIN
COURSE, OR
4 AS A FIRST
COURSE

What is a soft-shell crab? It's an ordinary blue crab that has shed its hard outer shell during the normal process of seasonal growth. The crabs have an entirely different taste when they are in this state, and the delicate soft shells add a nice crunch, especially when sautéed quickly. The peak of the soft-shell crab season is in July and August. Save yourself extra fuss by having the crabs cleaned at the fish market. Colorful Coleslaw (page 84) and tiny roast potatoes round out this meal.

 A CRISP AND SNAPPY WHITE—SOAVE, DRY RIESLING, MEDIUM- TO LIGHTWEIGHT CHARDONNAY, AUSTRALIAN SEMILLON—PROVIDES JUST THE RIGHT BALANCE HERE.

1. To make the coating, in a shallow medium dish, stir together all the ingredients.
2. Remove the feelers underneath the crab shells on both sides. Rinse the crabs and dry carefully.
3. In a large skillet over medium heat, melt the butter with the vegetable oil. Add the shallot and sauté until slightly softened, about 1 minute.
4. Roll the crabs in the flour mixture and place them in the skillet. Sauté, turning once, for about 3 minutes on each side. When they have finished cooking and have turned pink, add the lemon juice, garlic, parsley, and salt and pepper to taste and cook for another minute or two. Make sure the garlic is cooked but not browned. Taste for seasoning.
5. Transfer the crabs to individual plates and garnish with lemon and parsley. Serve immediately.

Coating

¼ cup all-purpose flour

pinch of freshly ground black pepper

pinch of salt

⅛ teaspoon cayenne pepper

⅛ teaspoon paprika

8 soft-shell crabs

¼ cup (½ stick) unsalted butter

1 tablespoon vegetable oil

1 medium shallot, finely chopped

¼ cup fresh lemon juice

2 medium garlic cloves, minced

2 tablespoons finely chopped
      fresh parsley

salt and freshly ground black pepper

Garnish

lemon slices

fresh parsley sprigs

grilled whole bluefish
with lemon-dill butter

SERVES 4

Eastern bluefish, with its meaty richness, is especially delicious when grilled with an herb butter. If the fish is large, it's helpful to make a deep cut every 2 inches without cutting through the bone, so that after it is cooked it can be easily divided into serving portions with a spatula. A wire grilling basket is useful for maneuvering the fish on the grill. Start with Bruschetta with Tomato, Basil, and Mozzarella (page 29) and serve Orzo with Goat Cheese (page 72) on the side. Strawberry Shortcake with Raspberry Custard Sauce (page 161) is a perfect ending.

 BLUEFISH IS RICH AND OILY AND NEEDS A BIG, OAKY CHARDONNAY FOR BALANCE. OR YOU MIGHT POUR A CRISP SAUVIGNON BLANC TO PROVIDE CONTRAST.

1. Prepare the barbecue for medium-high heat grilling.
2. To make the butter, in a small bowl, cream the butter until soft. Add the shallot, dill, garlic, lemon juice, lemon zest, salt to taste, and cayenne pepper and mix well. Taste for seasoning.
3. Season the bluefish with salt and pepper. Spoon about half the butter into the cavity of the bluefish. Arrange the dill and lemon slices over the butter in the cavity. Spread more butter over the outer surfaces of the fish.
4. Place the fish in a large grilling basket, if available. If not, be sure to place the fish on the grill carefully. Cover and grill about 3 inches from the fire, turning once, until just tender when pierced with a skewer, 8 to 10 minutes on each side.
5. Serve immediately with the remaining butter.

Advance Preparation: The butter may be prepared 3 days in advance and refrigerated.

Lemon-Dill Butter

½ cup (1 stick) unsalted butter,
    at room temperature

1 medium shallot, finely chopped

2 tablespoons finely chopped
    fresh dill

1 medium garlic clove, minced

2 tablespoons fresh lemon juice

1 teaspoon minced lemon zest

salt

pinch of cayenne pepper

1 whole bluefish, 3 to 4 pounds,
    cleaned and head removed

salt and freshly ground black pepper

1 bunch fresh dill

2 lemons, thinly sliced

chicken chili

SERVES 10-12

Marlene Sorosky, the noted cookbook author, introduced me to the idea of using chicken in chili. I prefer it to the beef versions during the hot summer months because it is lighter. I like to serve the chili on cool evenings to a large crowd when I want a substantial and informal main course. Serve with your favorite corn bread and a green salad. Put out a big bowl of Guacamole Salsa (page 30) to start and serve chilled Mexican beer.

 THIS SPICY DISH WOULD BLEND WELL WITH GEWÜRZTRAMINER, BUT BEER MAY BE THE BEST ACCOMPANIMENT.

1. Fill a large, deep pan three-fourths full with water and bring to a boil. Place the chicken breasts in the boiling water and turn off the heat. Cover and let sit for 25 minutes. Remove the chicken, cool, skin, and cube into 1-inch pieces. Cover and refrigerate. Remove from the refrigerator 30 minutes before adding to the chili.

2. In a 6-quart saucepan over medium heat, warm 3 tablespoons of the vegetable oil. Add the onions and sauté until softened, 3 to 5 minutes. Add the jalapeño chile and sauté for another minute. Add the garlic, oregano, cumin, coriander, cinnamon, and chili powder and stir until well combined.

3. Add the beer, chicken stock, and tomatoes and bring to a low simmer. Cover partially and simmer, stirring occasionally, until the sauce is very slightly thickened, about 1 hour.

4. Add the kidney and pinto beans to the chili mixture and continue simmering, uncovered, for 30 more minutes. The sauce should be slightly thickened.

5. Meanwhile, in a medium skillet over medium heat, warm the remaining 2 tablespoons oil. Add the red and yellow peppers and sauté until slightly cooked but still crisp, 3 to 5 minutes.

6 medium whole chicken breasts, boned

5 tablespoons vegetable oil

3 large onions, finely chopped

1 jalapeño chile, seeded and finely chopped (see note)

8 medium garlic cloves, finely minced

4 teaspoons ground oregano

3 tablespoons ground cumin

2 teaspoons ground coriander

1 teaspoon ground cinnamon

½ cup chili powder

2 cans (12 ounces each) beer

2½ cups chicken stock

1 can (28 ounces) crushed tomatoes

1 can (15 ounces) kidney beans, drained

1 can (16 ounces) pinto beans, drained

6. Add the chicken, sautéed peppers, grated chocolate, and salt to taste and stir until the chocolate is melted. Taste for seasoning.

7. Ladle into large chili or pottery bowls. Serve the garnishes—sour cream, salsa, Cheddar cheese, onions—in small bowls for guests to add as desired.

Advance Preparation: This may be prepared 3 days in advance through step 5 and refrigerated. Cover the chicken and the peppers separately and refrigerate. Remove from the refrigerator 1 hour before completing the dish.

Note: When working with chilies, always wear rubber gloves. Wash the cutting surface and knife immediately afterward.

2 red sweet peppers, seeded and cut
into ½-inch dice

1 yellow sweet pepper, seeded and
cut into ½-inch dice

1 square (1 ounce) unsweetened
chocolate, grated

salt

Garnish

sour cream

tomato salsa or jalapeño salsa

shredded sharp Cheddar cheese

chopped scallions or red onion

in tomatillo sauce
chicken

SERVES 4–6

You can make this dish as mild or hot as you like. For the mild version use the gentle Anaheim chile; for the hot version use the spicier poblano. Both must be roasted, peeled, and seeded before they are added to the sauce. Ground cumin seed gives an exotic taste that marries well with the Mexican tomatillo. If you are unable to find fresh chilies, the canned ones will do. This sauce is also good on grilled or poached chicken. For a Mexican-style dinner, start with Guacamole Salsa (page 30) with tortilla chips. Serve the chicken with grilled corn.

 SERVE A CRISP, FRUITY SAUVIGNON BLANC. THE WINE'S HERBAL CHARACTER MATCHES THE PEPPERS NICELY.

1. To peel the chilies, place on a broiler pan and broil approximately 6 inches from the heat until blackened on all sides. Use tongs to turn.

2. Slip the chilies into a brown paper bag and close tightly. Let rest for 10 minutes.

3. Remove the chilies from the bag, drain, and peel. Make a slit in each chile and open it up. Core, cut off the stem, and scrape out the seeds and ribs. Chop the chilies into ¼-inch pieces.

4. In a large sauté pan over medium-high heat, warm half of the vegetable oil. Add the chicken pieces and sauté, turning once, until lightly browned, 3 to 5 minutes on each side. You may have to do this in batches, adding the remaining oil as needed. Transfer to a platter.

5. Add the onion and sauté over medium heat until softened but not brown, 3 to 5 minutes.

6. Add the chicken stock, raise the heat, and deglaze the pan, scraping the browned bits off the bottom.

7. Add the garlic, chilies, tomatillos, cilantro, and cumin. Bring to a boil, then reduce the heat to low. Add the browned chicken pieces, cover, and cook, turning the chicken once to cook evenly, until just done, about 20 minutes. The smaller pieces will cook more quickly, so you will need to remove throughout.

3 medium Anaheim or poblano chilies (see note)

¼ cup vegetable oil

1 chicken fryer, about 3½ pounds, cut into serving pieces

2 medium whole chicken breasts, halved and skinned

1 large onion, finely chopped

2 cups chicken stock

6 medium garlic cloves, minced

1½ pounds tomatillos, husks removed, quartered

3 tablespoons finely chopped fresh cilantro

½ teaspoon ground cumin

8. Transfer the chicken to a serving platter and cover with aluminum foil to keep warm.

9. Add the lime juice to the pan and cook until the sauce reduces and is slightly thickened. Season with salt and pepper.

10. Pour the sauce over the chicken pieces and garnish with the cilantro leaves. Serve immediately.

Advance Preparation: This may be prepared 2 days in advance and refrigerated. Return to room temperature before reheating.

Note: When working with chilies always wear rubber gloves. Wash the cutting surface and knife immediately afterward.

2 tablespoons fresh lime juice

salt and freshly ground black pepper

Garnish

fresh cilantro leaves

wine temperature

Most Americans drink white wines too cold and red wines too warm. In the summer it is quite acceptable to chill Chardonnays and other whites, but too much cold will shut down their flavor. Keep them at around 55°F, no less. A half hour in the refrigerator is time enough to cool your wine; more than that will take the edge off the flavor. As for reds, it is perfectly fine to pop them into the refrigerator for 15 minutes or so, especially on hot days. Beaujolais and Zinfandel are particularly good when cooled down to 60° or 65°F. A slight chill can add a refreshing dimension to other reds, too, but don't get carried away.

sautéed chicken
with tomato-leek sauce

SERVES 4

I like to serve this dish at small dinner parties because I can make it in the morning when it's cool and reheat it while I'm entertaining my guests. The tomato-leek sauce, with its thyme and red pepper flakes, is a bold addition to the chicken. Sautéed Zucchini and Arugula (page 137) makes an appropriate accompaniment.

 A BIG, FULL-BODIED CHARDONNAY OR A VELVETY, YOUNG CABERNET SAUVIGNON COMPLEMENTS THIS DISH.

1. If using bacon, immerse in boiling water for 30 seconds to rid it of its smoky flavor before browning. In a medium skillet over medium-high heat, melt 1 tablespoon of the butter with 1 tablespoon of the olive oil. Add the pancetta or bacon and fry until browned, 3 to 5 minutes. Using a slotted spoon, transfer to paper towels to drain.

2. Add the remaining 1 tablespoon each butter and olive oil to the pan over medium-high heat. Add the chicken and sauté, turning once, until nicely browned, 5 to 7 minutes on each side. Remove to a platter and cover with aluminum foil to keep warm. Discard all but 2 tablespoons of the fat from the pan.

3. Add the leeks to the pan and sauté over medium-high heat until softened, 3 to 5 minutes.

4. Add the tomatoes, reduce the heat to medium, and cook until the tomatoes are softened, 3 to 5 minutes.

5. Add the chicken stock, cream, and tomato paste and raise the heat to medium-high. Reduce by one-fourth, or until slightly thickened. Stir in the thyme, red pepper flakes, and salt to taste.

6. Return the chicken breasts and pancetta to the sauce and heat over medium heat until warmed through, about 5 minutes. Taste for seasoning.

7. Transfer to platter and garnish each breast with thyme sprigs. Serve immediately.

Advance Preparation: This may be prepared 8 hours in advance through step 5 and refrigerated. Return to room temperature before reheating.

¼ pound pancetta or bacon, cut into ¼-inch dice

2 tablespoons unsalted butter

2 tablespoons olive oil

2 large whole chicken breasts, boned, skinned, halved and pounded evenly

2 medium leeks, white part only, finely chopped

2 medium tomatoes, peeled, seeded, and finely chopped

½ cup chicken stock

¼ cup whipping cream

1 teaspoon tomato paste

2 teaspoons finely chopped fresh thyme

pinch of red pepper flakes

salt

Garnish

fresh thyme sprigs

grilled**chicken**

with sun-dried-tomato marinade

SERVES 4–6

Basil, olive oil, mustard, and sun-dried tomatoes combine to make a thick marinade that forms a crisp mahogany crust on the chicken as it grills. I prefer to use dry-packed sun-dried tomatoes, since they are about a quarter the price of the imported Italian oil-packed variety. Serve the chicken to friends who like a little extra spice at the table.

 THIS FULL-FLAVORED DISH DOES NICELY WITH FRUITY REDS SUCH AS BEAUJOLAIS OR GAMAY.

1. To make the marinade, place the sun-dried tomatoes in a small heatproof bowl and pour in the boiling water. Let soften for 15 to 30 minutes. Drain well.

2. Mince the garlic in a food processor. Add the drained tomatoes, olive oil, red pepper flakes, mustard, vinegar, and salt and pepper to taste. Process until a thick, smooth paste forms. Transfer marinade to a small bowl.

3. In the processor, combine the butter with 2 tablespoons of the marinade and process until well blended. Transfer the mixture to a sheet of waxed paper and roll up into a cylinder. Refrigerate for at least 4 hours or until ready to use. It should become very firm.

4. Place the chicken breasts in large, shallow nonaluminum dish and coat evenly with the marinade paste. Make sure to slip some marinade under the skin. Cover and refrigerate for at least 2 hours or as long as 8 hours, turning the chicken pieces several times to make sure the marinade is adhering to them. (The longer it marinates, the spicier it will be.)

5. Prepare the barbecue for medium-heat grilling.

6. Grill the chicken 3 inches from the fire, turning once, until done, 7 to 10 minutes on each side, basting each side with a thin slice of the butter mixture.

7. To serve, transfer the chicken pieces to individual plates and top each piece with a thin slice of the butter.

Advance Preparation: This may be prepared 8 hours in advance through step 4.

Marinade Paste

¾ cup dry-packed sun-dried
    tomatoes
boiling water, to cover
4 medium garlic cloves
1 teaspoon extra-virgin olive oil
1 teaspoon red pepper flakes
2 tablespoons Dijon mustard
2 tablespoons balsamic vinegar
salt and freshly ground black pepper

¼ cup (½ stick) unsalted butter,
    at room temperature
3 large whole chicken breasts,
    boned, halved, and flattened

grilled**mexican**chicken

with citrus yogurt sauce

SERVES 6

Overnight marinating is the secret to locking in the flavor and producing this tender, succulent chicken. I like to serve it for informal outdoor dinners with family and friends. Start with Three-Lettuce Salad with Tomato-Tarragon Dressing (page 78) and serve the chicken with Cracked Wheat–Vegetable Salad (page 86). Dessert calls for Hazelnut-Plum Tart (page 169) with a bowl of crème fraîche on the side.

 TRY A BIG, FRUITY CHARDONNAY OR A SPICY GEWÜRZTRAMINER.

1. To make the marinade, in a bowl large enough to hold the chicken, stir together all the ingredients. Taste for seasoning.
2. Measure out 1 cup of the marinade, cover, and refrigerate for the sauce.
3. Place the chicken pieces in the bowl and, using your hands, evenly coat them with the marinade. Cover and refrigerate overnight or as long as 24 hours for the best flavor, turning occasionally.
4. Prepare the barbecue for medium-heat grilling.
5. Remove the chicken from the marinade and grill 3 inches from the fire, turning once, or until done, 7 to 12 minutes on each side, depending on size.
6. Transfer to a serving platter and garnish with orange and lemon slices and parsley. Serve immediately with the reserved sauce.

Advance Preparation: This may be prepared 1 day in advance through step 5 and refrigerated. Serve cold.

Marinade

2 cups plain low-fat yogurt

2 medium shallots, finely chopped

3 medium garlic cloves, minced

¼ cup fresh orange juice

2 tablespoons fresh lime juice

2 tablespoons finely chopped
    fresh cilantro

½ teaspoon ground cumin

salt and freshly ground white pepper

3 medium whole chicken
    breasts, halved

1 fryer chicken, about 3½ pounds,
    cut into serving pieces

Garnish

2 oranges, sliced

2 lemons, sliced

1 bunch fresh parsley

grilledmarinatedchicken

SERVES 4–6

This winning combination of grilled chicken and savory mustard, sweet wine, and aromatic tarragon is light and easy to prepare for last-minute cooking. Serve with Herbed New Potatoes with Vermouth (page 154).

 THE RICH PORT AND PEPPER FLAVORS NEED A HEARTY RED WINE SUCH AS A RIPE ZINFANDEL OR A SPICY RHÔNE.

1. To make the marinade, in a small bowl, whisk together all the ingredients, mixing well.
2. Place the chicken pieces in a large, shallow nonaluminum dish, pour the marinade over them, and turn to coat evenly. Cover and marinate for at least 30 minutes or as long as 4 hours in the refrigerator.
3. Prepare the barbecue for medium-heat grilling.
4. Remove the chicken from the marinade and grill 3 inches from the fire, turning once, until done, 7 to 10 minutes on each side, depending on size.
5. Transfer the chicken to individual plates, garnish with the tarragon leaves, and serve.

Advance Preparation: This may be prepared 4 hours in advance through step 2 and refrigerated.

Marinade

½ cup Dijon mustard

½ cup port

2 tablespoons finely chopped
   fresh tarragon

freshly ground black pepper

3 large whole chicken breasts,
   boned and halved

Garnish

fresh tarragon leaves

roasted rosemary-lemon chicken

SERVES 4

Perfectly cooked, fragrant chicken can be served at nearly any temperature and for nearly any occasion. In this recipe, the chicken is split and flattened for even cooking. If you are pressed for time, ask your butcher to ready the chicken for roasting. Rosemary is tucked underneath the skin to infuse the bird with its distinctive aroma. Accompany the chicken with an array of your favorite grilled vegetables and Light Summer Pasta (page 66).

 ROSEMARY AND CHICKEN WORK VERY WELL WITH BIG, OAKY CHARDONNAYS.

1. Rinse the chicken halves and pat dry. With the side of a heavy cleaver, flatten each half by pounding hard a few times.

2. Separate the skin from each chicken half by carefully slipping your fingers under the skin and gently loosening it. Tuck as many rosemary leaves as you like under the skin, then pat the skin back into place.

3. To make the marinade, in a large bowl, thoroughly whisk together all the ingredients, including salt and pepper to taste.

4. Place the chicken in a bowl with the marinade and rotate until completely coated. Cover and marinate for at least 2 hours or as long as 4 hours in the refrigerator.

5. Preheat the oven to 425°F.

6. Remove the chicken from the marinade, reserving the marinade, and place on a roasting rack in a roasting pan. Pour the water into the pan. Roast the chicken, basting a few times with the reserved marinade, until golden brown and the juices run clear, 45 to 50 minutes. If the pan begins to burn, add more water to it.

7. Transfer the chicken to a platter. Serve hot, at room temperature, or slightly chilled.

Advance Preparation: This may be completely prepared 2 days in advance and refrigerated. It is excellent served at room temperature or slightly chilled.

1 fryer chicken, 3½ pounds, split

1 small bunch fresh rosemary sprigs

Marinade

2 teaspoons finely chopped
     fresh rosemary

3 medium garlic cloves, minced

¼ cup fresh lemon juice

¼ cup olive oil

1 teaspoon soy sauce

salt

¼ teaspoon cayenne pepper

1 cup water

crispy roasted chicken

with spinach pesto cream

SERVES 6–8

Guests always rave about this dish. Roast the chicken while your guests are enjoying their drinks and first course. The smell of the pesto-marinated chickens cooking in the oven sweetens the air. I've suggested garnishing the platter with purple and green basil leaves and flowers. If you have access to society garlic flowers, they make a spectacular addition. ✳ *Layering flavors is a cooking technique that infuses the food with a particular flavor at each successive step. This chicken is first marinated with a pesto base and then stuffed with pesto-flavored bread crumbs. Finally, cream and pesto are blended together for a smooth sauce that is poured over the hot, crispy chicken. Although a triple taste of pesto may sound excessive, it is actually an ideal balance.* ✳ *For a large dinner party, start with Corn-Leek Cakes with Caviar, Smoked Salmon, and Crème Fraîche (page 36). If you serve the chicken on a buffet, accompany it with large platters of Chilled Asparagus with Red Pepper Vinaigrette (page 144), Cracked Wheat–Vegetable Salad (page 86), and Garden Salad with Goat Cheese–Thyme Dressing (page 80). Serve loaves of country French bread and crocks of sweet butter. Prepare a dessert sideboard of Poached Peaches in White Zinfandel with Raspberry Sauce (page 156); Lattice Crust Pie with Rhubarb, Peaches, Strawberries, and Plums (page 165); and Chocolate Pecan Torte with Espresso Crème Anglaise (page 171).*

 THE COMPLEX FLAVORS OF THIS DISH ARE NICELY HIGHLIGHTED BY A WELL-BALANCED AND FAIRLY YOUNG CABERNET SAUVIGNON OR MERLOT.

1. To make the sauce, in a small bowl, whisk together all the ingredients, including salt and pepper to taste.
2. To make the marinade, in a small bowl, whisk together all the ingredients, including salt and pepper to taste, and mix well.
3. Arrange the chicken breasts in a large, shallow nonaluminum dish. Pour the marinade over the chicken, turning to coat generously. Cover and marinate for at least 30 minutes or as long as 4 hours in the refrigerator.
4. To make the stuffing, in a medium bowl, combine all the ingredients, including salt and pepper to taste, and mix until the pesto has been absorbed.
5. Preheat the oven to 425°F.
6. Remove the chicken breasts from the marinade and place in a large roasting pan, skin side up. Separate the skin from each chicken breast by carefully slipping your fingers under the skin and gently loosening it.

Sauce

½ cup Spinach Pesto (page 192)

1 tablespoon red wine vinegar

½ cup crème fraîche

Salt and freshly ground black pepper

Marinade

¼ cup dry white wine

¼ cup Spinach Pesto (page 192)

salt and freshly ground black pepper

recipe continues ▶

7. Place a heaping tablespoon of stuffing underneath the skin. Pat the skin back into place, pressing gently.

8. Place the chicken breasts in the oven and roast for 20 to 25 minutes. They should be golden brown and crisp. If not, remove them from the oven and turn the oven to broil. Broil the chicken breasts until the skin is very crisp, 3 to 5 minutes.

9. Transfer the chicken breasts to a platter and spoon 1 tablespoon of the sauce onto each breast. Garnish with basil sprigs and flowers and serve immediately. Serve the remaining sauce on the side.

Advance Preparation: The sauce may be prepared 1 day in advance and refrigerated. Remove from the refrigerator 30 minutes before serving. The marinade may also be prepared 1 day in advance and refrigerated. Remove from the refrigerator 1 hour before using.

Stuffing

1 cup fresh bread crumbs

3 tablespoons freshly grated
 Parmesan cheese

2 tablespoons Spinach Pesto
 (page 192)

salt and freshly ground black pepper

4 large whole chicken breasts,
 about 1¾ pounds each, boned
 and halved

Garnish

purple and green basil leaves
 and flowers

barbecued leg of lamb

SERVES 8–10

Pineapple sage is one of my favorite seasonings. Rich with a fragrant, musty taste and the fruitiness of ripe pineapple, the herb was my inspiration for this recipe. If you don't have pineapple sage, however, any sage will do. ✳ *Here, the whole leg of lamb is boned and butterflied, then pounded into a uniform thickness so that it will cook more evenly. It is marinated overnight in red wine and olive oil with plenty of fresh sage. Before cooking, a savory coating of mustard and sage is applied that becomes a delectable crust when grilled. Finally, a sauce of veal stock and sage is spooned over the medium-rare lamb slices. It is best to use a covered gas grill for this recipe. If you love lamb chops, try grilling them with this marinade and mustard crust for a quicker version.* ✳ *This is an ideal dinner-party dish. Begin with Stuffed Baby Red Potatoes with Eggplant, Tomato, and Peppers (page 39), followed by Garden Salad with Goat Cheese–Thyme Dressing (page 80). Serve the lamb with Assorted Grilled Vegetable Platter (page 138) or Spicy Capellini with Summer Vegetables (page 68). For dessert, serve Chocolate Pecan Torte with Espresso Crème Anglaise (page 171).*

USE A GOOD-QUALITY CABERNET IN COOKING (IT MAY NOT SEEM SO, BUT IT IS EASY TO TELL WHEN A POOR OR MEDIOCRE WINE IS USED IN PREPARING A DISH), AND SERVE THE SAME WINE WITH DINNER.

1. To make the marinade, in a small nonaluminum bowl, combine all the ingredients, including salt and pepper to taste, mixing well. Measure out ½ cup, cover, and refrigerate until making the sauce.

2. Lay the leg of lamb flat in a large, shallow nonaluminum pan and pour the marinade over it, making sure it is evenly distributed. Cover and refrigerate, turning occasionally to marinate evenly, for at least 8 hours or preferably for 1 day.

3. When ready to grill, prepare the coating: In a small bowl, stir together the mustard, sage, and pepper to taste. Slowly whisk in the olive oil.

4. Prepare the barbecue for medium-high-heat grilling.

5. Remove the lamb from the marinade and pat dry. Place on a large platter and, using your hands, coat both sides with the mustard coating. Place the lamb on the grill about 3 inches from the fire and sear on both sides, about 3 minutes on each side. Turn down the barbecue to medium heat. Cover and grill, turning once, for 20 to 25 minutes on each side. You may need to cut a piece off that is cooked before the rest of the lamb is ready if the leg is much thicker in certain places. The meat should be very pink

Marinade

3 large shallots, finely chopped

2 medium garlic cloves, minced

1 cup Cabernet Sauvignon or other full-bodied red wine

¼ cup olive oil

¼ cup finely chopped fresh sage, preferably pineapple sage, or 2 tablespoons dried sage

salt and freshly ground black pepper

1 leg of lamb with sirloin attached, 9 to 10 pounds, boned, butterflied, and evenly flattened (5 to 6 pounds boned)

recipe continues ▶

inside. To test, insert an instant-read thermometer in the thickest part of the leg; it should read 140°F for medium-rare or 150°F for medium.

6. Meanwhile, make the sauce: Pour the reserved marinade and the stock into a small saucepan. Bring to a boil over high heat and boil until reduced to about ½ cup. It should be slightly thickened. Just before serving, with the pan over medium-high heat, add the sage and then the butter, whisking it in slowly so that the sauce becomes slightly shiny. Taste for seasoning.

7. Transfer the lamb to a wooden carving platter and let rest for about 10 minutes. Slice against the grain and serve with a little sauce poured over each portion. Garnish with sage sprigs, if available.

Advance Preparation: This may be prepared 1 day in advance through step 2 and refrigerated.

Coating

½ cup whole-grain mustard

3 tablespoons finely chopped fresh
    sage, or 1 tablespoon dried sage

freshly ground black pepper

3 tablespoons olive oil

Sauce

½ cup reserved marinade

1 cup veal or beef stock

1 tablespoon finely chopped fresh
    sage or 1½ teaspoons
    dried sage

2 tablespoons unsalted butter,
    at room temperature

Garnish

fresh sage sprigs (optional)

Despite the appearance of edible flowers on dinner plates all over the country, I prefer eating tasty herb blossoms to munching on rose petals. I like to garnish dishes with the flowers of the herb the dish contains. I also like to sprinkle several different herb blossoms over simple green salads. Pick the blossoms just before serving, if possible. Otherwise, refrigerate them; they will keep for as long as a week. These are not just pretty garnishes, however. If you've never tasted herb flowers, you have a real pleasure in store. Some of my favorites are:

Arugula—creamy white flowers with a dash each
of black and red near the center
Green or purple basil—spiked blossoms of the same color
Borage—blue–purplish pink flowers
Garlic chive—white flowers
Society garlic—purple flowers
Lavender—purple wands
Oregano—tiny mauve-and-white flowers
Rosemary—tiny, bright sky blue flowers
Pineapple sage—scarlet flowers
Thyme—tiny purple flowers

herb flowers

barbecued brisket of beef

SERVES 6–8

Brisket needs long, slow cooking to become tender. Here it is roasted and then sliced before it goes near the grill. This is a wonderful dish for a celebration like Memorial Day or the Fourth of July because you can roast it a few days before your party. After slicing the meat, place it on heavy-duty aluminum foil and spoon on the barbecue sauce. Seal the packet by double folding the edges. When ready to eat, simply warm the brisket in the packets on the grill. The barbecue sauce, with its chipotle chilies and adobo sauce, is also great on sandwiches. Your favorite baked beans, Colorful Coleslaw (page 84), and Herbed Garlic Cheese Bread (page 41) make perfect side dishes. Start with Roasted Eggplant with Balsamic Vinegar (page 35). For dessert, serve Strawberry Shortcake with Raspberry Custard Sauce (page 161).

 A FINE, COMPLEX CABERNET SAUVIGNON, MERLOT, BARBARESCO, OR ZINFANDEL IS THE RIGHT CHOICE FOR THIS HEARTY DISH.

1. Preheat the oven to 325°F.

2. Season the brisket with salt and pepper on both sides. Place in a roasting pan, add the stock, and cover. Roast until tender when pierced with a fork, 3 to 4 hours. The timing will depend on the size of the brisket.

3. Remove the brisket from the oven. Pour off the juices from the pan and reserve. Cover the pan with aluminum foil and let the meat cool.

4. Slice the cooled brisket against the grain into ¼-inch-thick slices and place on a sheet of heavy-duty aluminum foil. Bring up the sides and seal tightly. Set aside until ready to finish cooking.

5. While the brisket is cooking, make the sauce: In a large saucepan over medium heat, warm the vegetable oil. Add the onion and sauté until lightly browned, about 5 minutes. Add the garlic and cook for another minute. Add all the remaining ingredients, including salt and pepper to taste, reduce the heat to medium-low, and simmer, uncovered, until the sauce is slightly thickened, 15 to 20 minutes. Remove the lemon slices and discard. Add the reserved juices from the roasted brisket and stir well. Taste for seasoning.

1 beef brisket, 4 to 5 pounds

salt and freshly ground black pepper

2 cups chicken stock

Sauce

1 tablespoon vegetable oil

1 large onion, finely chopped

3 garlic cloves, minced

1 can (6 ounces) tomato paste

2 cups apple cider

1 tablespoon soy sauce

2 tablespoons cider vinegar

1 tablespoon molasses

1 tablespoon plus 2 teaspoons
   Dijon mustard

6. When ready to finish cooking, prepare the barbecue for medium-heat grilling. (If the barbecue is too hot, the bottom of the meat will burn.) Open the foil packet and generously brush the brisket slices with some of the sauce. Close the foil tightly, making sure there are no holes or openings.

7. Place the brisket package on the grill, cover, and grill until the sauce is bubbling and the meat is heated through, 10 to 15 minutes. (If the fire gets too hot, you may need to open the vents to control it.)

8. Remove the brisket slices from the foil and arrange on a platter. Serve with the remaining barbecue sauce.

9. If making sandwiches, toast the halved French rolls on the grill just until hot. Arrange the brisket slices on half of a roll, spoon on some sauce, and cover with the other half. Serve immediately.

Advance Preparation: The brisket may be prepared 2 days in advance through step 5. Refrigerate the brisket and the sauce separately. Remove from the refrigerator 1 hour before barbecuing the brisket.

½ to 1 chipotle chile in adobo sauce, or to taste, finely chopped, plus ¼ teaspoon adobo sauce

2 lemon slices

salt and freshly ground pepper to taste

8 French rolls, split (optional)

grilledmarinatedflanksteak

SERVES 4–6

Flank steaks need to be tenderized by pounding, slow cooking, or marinating. Here, red wine, citrus, and curry make a flavorful marinade. Grill the steak until just medium-rare, as further cooking will toughen the meat. It is great to have on hand for building weekend sandwiches; spread French rolls with mayonnaise flavored with Ancho Chile Paste (page 195) and top with slices of flank steak, sliced ripe tomatoes, and arugula leaves.

 A HEARTY RED SUCH AS A ZINFANDEL, CÔTES DU RHÔNE, PETITE SYRAH, OR CHARBONO IS JUST RIGHT HERE.

1. To make the marinade, in a medium bowl, combine all the ingredients and whisk until well combined. Taste for seasoning.
2. Lay out the flank steak flat in a large, shallow nonaluminum dish. Pour the marinade over, turn to coat evenly, cover, and marinate for at least 2 hours or as long as 4 hours in the refrigerator.
3. Prepare the barbecue for medium-heat grilling.
4. Remove the steak from the marinade and grill 3 inches from the fire, turning once, for 5 to 7 minutes on each side for medium-rare.
5. Transfer to a wooden carving platter and slice thinly against the grain. Place on a serving platter and serve immediately.

Advance Preparation: This may be prepared up to 4 hours in advance through step 2 and refrigerated. If serving cold, it may be completely prepared 1 day in advance and refrigerated.

Marinade

¾ cup red wine

2 medium garlic cloves, minced

2 tablespoons olive oil

1 tablespoon fresh lemon juice

2 tablespoons fresh orange juice

1 teaspoon grated orange zest

1 teaspoon grated lemon zest

1 teaspoon soy sauce

½ teaspoon curry powder

salt and freshly ground black pepper

1 flank steak, about 2 pounds

california style
grilled steaks

SERVES 4

When I was a child, teriyaki-marinated steaks were staple summer fare. This simple marinade is an updated version, still using soy sauce but adding balsamic vinegar for its musty, sweet flavor. Serve with Broiled Tomatoes Glazed with Mustard-Herb Mayonnaise (page 140) for a speedy—and delicious—dinner. A good ending is Frozen Praline Mousse (page 173) with Bittersweet Hot Fudge Sauce (page 177) or, if you are in a hurry, your favorite ice cream.

 DRINK YOUR BEST CABERNET SAUVIGNON OR MERLOT WITH THIS DISH.

1. To make the marinade, in a small bowl, thoroughly whisk together all the ingredients, including pepper to taste.
2. Arrange the steaks in a single layer in a shallow nonaluminum dish. Pour the marinade over steaks, turn to coat evenly, cover, and marinate for at least 2 to as long as 4 hours in the refrigerator.
3. Prepare the barbecue for medium-high-heat grilling.
4. Grill or broil the steaks about 3 inches from the fire, turning once, about 4 minutes on each side for rare, or to desired doneness.
5. Transfer to individual plates and serve immediately.

Advance Preparation: This may be prepared 4 hours in advance through step 2 and refrigerated.

Marinade

2 medium garlic cloves, finely chopped

2 medium shallots, finely chopped

2 tablespoons soy sauce

1/4 cup balsamic vinegar

2 tablespoons olive oil

freshly ground black pepper

4 Spencer, sirloin, or New York steaks, 1/2 to 3/4 pound each

✳ grilling ahead

Although grilled foods are traditionally served hot off the fire, they taste every bit as good— and maybe even better on a very hot day—several hours later. Bypassing all the drama of the split-second timing required to prepare hot grilled food, this method gives you all of the pleasures and none of the aggravation of cooking in front of your guests. Almost all of the grilled main courses—red meats, poultry, fish, vegetables—in this book may be served at room temperature or just slightly chilled.

sweetandhotspareribs
with apricot-plum sauce

SERVES 4

Barbecued ribs are an American institution. I use either the individually cut Chinese-style baby back ribs for their meatiness or the slab baby back ribs. The sweet and hot sauce is made by simmering fruit with garlic, ginger, and red pepper flakes. The result is a spicy, chutneylike flavor. Baking the ribs first ensures a perfectly cooked and moist result. Serve extra Apricot-Plum Sauce (page 194) on the side. This is a particularly good choice for a Fourth of July celebration. Colorful Coleslaw (page 84) and Grilled Corn on the Cob with Ancho Chile Butter (page 146) complete the meal.

 GEWÜRZTRAMINER IS FINE WITH THIS DISH. A MORE DARING IMBIBER CAN POUR A SPICY ZINFANDEL.

1. To make the marinade, in a bowl, stir together the white wine and Apricot-Plum Sauce, blending well.
2. Place the ribs in a jumbo lock-top plastic bag. Add one-half of the marinade to the ribs, seal closed, and marinate in the refrigerator for at least 2 hours or as long as 8 hours, turning occasionally. Cover and reserve the remaining marinade in the refrigerator, to use as a basting sauce.
3. Preheat the oven to 325°F.
4. Place the ribs and excess marinade on a large sheet of aluminum foil. Bring up the sides and seal closed, being careful not to pierce the foil. Place the package in a large roasting pan and bake for 1 hour.
5. Meanwhile, prepare the barbecue for medium-heat grilling.
6. Remove the ribs from the oven. Unwrap the ribs, drain, and place in a dish to cool slightly.
7. Grill the ribs about 3 inches from the fire, turning once and basting occasionally with the reserved marinade, until crisp and brown, 5 to 7 minutes on each side.
8. Transfer to a serving platter and serve with the Apricot-Plum Sauce.

Advance Preparation: This may be prepared 8 hours ahead through step 6 and refrigerated. Remove from the refrigerator 30 minutes before grilling.

Marinade

1 cup fruity white wine such as Gewürztraminer, Johannisberg Riesling, or Chenin Blanc

1 cup Apricot-Plum Sauce (page 194)

4 pounds pork loin ribs, cut Chinese style or baby back ribs (see introduction)

For serving

1 cup Apricot-Plum Sauce (page 194)

with grilled summer salsa
grilledvealchops

SERVES 6

Veal chops taste best grilled medium-rare. In the colder months, complex mushroom sauces are a wonderful counterpoint to the veal's delicate flavor. In the summer, this lively salsa is the perfect complement to the mild veal flavor. Serve Gratin of Summer Squash with Leeks and Rice (page 136) or Lemon-Herb Roasted Potatoes (page 152) for a satisfying meal. For dessert try Hazelnut-Plum Tart (page 169).

 SANGIOVESE, RHÔNE VARIETIES, AND PINOT NOIR ARE THE BEST CHOICES FOR THIS DELICIOUS DISH.

1. Prepare the barbecue for medium-heat grilling.

2. To make the salsa, place the zucchini, eggplant, and red onion slices on the grill 3 inches from the fire and grill, turning once, until slightly charred, about 4 minutes on each side.

3. Transfer the vegetables to a cutting board, chop into ¼-inch pieces, and place in a medium bowl.

4. Place the corn on the barbecue and grill it, turning the ear just as the kernels begin to darken. Remove the corn from the grill and let cool until it can be handled. Using a sharp knife, cut the kernels from the ear. Add to the bowl with the vegetables. Add all the remaining salsa ingredients, including salt and pepper to taste, and mix to combine. Taste for seasoning.

Salsa

2 medium zucchini, cut lengthwise into ¼-inch-thick slices

2 small Japanese eggplants, cut lengthwise into ¼-inch-thick slices

½ small red onion, cut into ¼-inch-thick slices (about 3 slices)

1 ear corn, husks and silk removed

1 garlic clove, minced

2 cups mixed red and yellow cherry tomatoes, finely diced

2 tablespoons olive oil

1 tablespoon balsamic vinegar

2 tablespoons finely chopped fresh basil

2 tablespoons finely chopped fresh parsley

salt and freshly ground black pepper

recipe continues

5. To make the glaze, in a small bowl, stir together all the ingredients. Brush the veal chops on both sides with the glaze.
6. Grill the veal about 3 inches from fire, turning once, for 5 to 7 minutes on each side. The veal should be very pink inside.
7. Transfer the veal chops to individual plates and spoon a large dollop of the salsa on the veal chops. Garnish each plate with basil or thyme leaves. Serve immediately.

Advance Preparation: This may be prepared 8 hours in advance through step 4. Refrigerate the veal chops and the salsa.

Glaze

3 tablespoons olive oil

2 tablespoons balsamic vinegar

1 shallot, finely chopped

1 garlic clove, minced

1 tablespoon finely chopped
 fresh thyme

salt and freshly ground black pepper

6 veal loin chops, 8 to 10 ounces each

Garnish

large fresh basil leaves or thyme leaves

fingerbowls

Whenever you serve grilled chicken, spareribs, or corn on the cob, everyone's hands will, of course, be a mess. To remedy the situation, put out individual fingerbowls—any small china or glass bowls—filled with warm water. Try one of the following suggestions to give this classic ritual a special touch:

- *Add a few drops of orange flower water to each bowl and float a thin slice of orange or lemon on top.*
- *Add a few drops of rosewater to each bowl and float rose petals on top.*
- *Place a sprig of fresh rosemary in each bowl, then pour warm water over the rosemary to release its powerful fragrance. The rosemary will float to the top.*
- *Accompany each bowl with a small cloth napkin, rolled up with a fresh herb sprig inside, to use as a hand towel.*

vegetables and other side dishes

gratinofsummersquash

with leeks and rice

SERVES 6

Sautéed leeks interlaced with colorful shredded summer squash and creamy rice contrast deliciously with sharp Parmesan cheese in this "all-in-one" vegetable dish. Serve as a side dish or a first course with Grilled Chicken with Sun-Dried-Tomato Marinade (page 115).

1. Using a food processor fitted with the shredder blade, shred the yellow and green zucchini. Place in a colander and add the salt, mixing until evenly distributed. Place the colander over a bowl and let drain for 15 to 30 minutes, capturing the juices in the bowl.

2. Wrap the zucchini in a clean dish towel and wring over the bowl to collect any additional juices. Set the juices aside and dry the squash well with a dry towel.

3. In a medium saucepan, bring the water to a boil. Add the rice, adjust the heat to simmer, and cook for 5 minutes. Drain and reserve.

4. Preheat the oven to 425°F.

5. In an 11-inch ovenproof pan or skillet over medium-high heat, warm 3 tablespoons of the olive oil. Add the leeks and sauté until slightly softened, about 5 minutes.

6. Add the remaining 1 tablespoon olive oil and the zucchini and sauté until almost tender, about 3 minutes. Add the garlic and parsley and sauté for another minute.

7. Sprinkle in the flour and stir over medium heat (a pasta fork works well) for 2 minutes. Remove from the heat and add the half-and-half and the squash liquid. Return to medium heat and continue to cook, stirring constantly, until slightly thickened, about 3 minutes.

8. Add the rice and all but 2 tablespoons of the Parmesan cheese and mix well. Season with salt and pepper. Sprinkle the remaining cheese on top.

9. Bake until browned and bubbling and the rice has absorbed the liquid, about 25 minutes. Serve immediately.

Advance Preparation: This may be prepared in the morning through step 8 (except for preheating the oven) and refrigerated. Bring to room temperature before baking.

2½ pounds mixed yellow and
   green zucchini

1 teaspoon salt

1½ cups water

½ cup long-grain white rice

¼ cup olive oil

3 medium leeks, white and light
   green parts only, finely chopped
   (about 3 cups)

2 medium garlic cloves, minced

2 tablespoons finely chopped fresh
   Italian parsley

2 tablespoons all-purpose flour

2 cups half-and-half

¾ cup freshly grated
   Parmesan cheese

salt and freshly ground black pepper

sautéedzucchiniandarugula

SERVES 4–6

Zesty, slightly bitter arugula gives this unusual vegetable sauté a pleasant tang. Serve it as an accompaniment to Sautéed Chicken with Tomato-Leek Sauce (page 114) or Grilled Swordfish with Herbed Green Sauce (page 96).

1. Place the zucchini in a dry dish towel and wring out all the excess moisture. Dry the squash carefully with a dry towel.
2. In a medium sauté pan over medium heat, melt the butter. Add the zucchini and stir for 2 minutes. Add the arugula and continue stirring for another minute or two. Add the garlic, lemon zest, lemon juice, and salt and pepper to taste. Stir until combined. Taste for seasoning. Serve immediately.

4 zucchini, about 1 pound,
   coarsely shredded

2 tablespoons unsalted butter

2 medium bunches arugula,
   finely shredded

1 medium garlic clove, minced

1 teaspoon grated lemon zest

1 tablespoon fresh lemon juice

salt and freshly ground black pepper

assortedgrilledvegetableplatter

SERVES 6

These colorful vegetables, branded with grill marks, make a wonderful side dish or even a first course. Be creative and select other fresh vegetables for grilling. Or you can use this technique to cook just one of the vegetables listed here. You can also omit the Summer Vinaigrette (page 182) and simply drizzle the vegetables with fresh lime or lemon juice and extra-virgin olive oil. A loaf of country French or olive bread makes a nice addition. A stunning salad can be created by chopping all of the grilled vegetables and combining them with grilled chicken, shrimp, or scallops.

1. Prepare the barbecue for medium-high heat grilling.
2. Place the peppers on the grill about 3 inches from the fire and grill, turning once with tongs, until the skin is blistered and slightly charred on all sides. Never pierce the pepper or the juices will escape. Put the peppers in a brown paper bag, close it tightly, and let stand for 10 minutes.
3. Remove the peppers from the bag, drain the peppers, and peel away the skins. Make a slit in each pepper, open it up flat, and remove the core, stem, seeds, and ribs. Cut lengthwise with a sharp knife or a pizza cutter into ½-inch-wide strips. Place on a serving platter.
4. Trim the stems off the zucchini and eggplants and cut them lengthwise into ¼-inch-thick slices. Spray the eggplant and zucchini slices with olive oil and grill on each side until the vegetables have grill marks and are beginning to feel soft, 3 to 4 minutes on each side. Transfer to a serving platter.
5. Repeat with the tomatoes, grilling them about 3 minutes on each side. Grill the asparagus, turning to cook evenly, for about 5 minutes total grilling time.
6. Arrange the vegetables on the platter in an attractive design. Serve at room temperature or cover and refrigerate until chilled.
7. Just before serving, drizzle the vegetables with the Summer Vinaigrette and garnish with the herbs.

Advance Preparation: This may be prepared 1 day ahead through step 6 and refrigerated.

2 red sweet peppers

2 yellow sweet peppers

4 medium zucchini

4 medium Japanese eggplants

olive oil nonstick cooking spray

6 plum (Roma) tomatoes,
    halved crosswise

12 asparagus, tough ends trimmed
    and spears peeled

½ cup Summer Vinaigrette
    (page 182)

Garnish

finely chopped mixed fresh herbs

broiled**tomatoes**

SERVES 6

Beautiful, ripe tomato halves or slices are brushed with a tangy mayonnaise topping, baked, and then broiled right before serving. These bubbly, golden brown tomatoes are excellent with Roasted Sea Bass with Herbs (page 100), Roasted Rosemary-Lemon Chicken (page 118), or Grilled Steaks, California Style (page 129).

1. Preheat the oven to 400°F.
2. Cut the tomatoes in half crosswise or into 1½-inch-thick slices. Place cut side up in a single layer in an ovenproof baking dish.
3. In a small bowl, stir together the mayonnaise, mustard, parsley, chives, 2 tablespoons of the Parmesan cheese, and salt and pepper to taste.
4. Spoon a heaping teaspoon of the mayonnaise mixture on top of each tomato, spreading to cover the top. Sprinkle the tomatoes with the remaining 1 tablespoon Parmesan cheese.
5. Bake until hot, 10 to 12 minutes; the time will depend on the size of the tomato slices or halves. Turn the oven to broil, move the tomatoes to the broiler, and brown until glazed and bubbling.
6. Remove from the oven and garnish with the parsley. Serve immediately.

Advance Preparation: This may be prepared up to 4 hours in advance through step 4 (except for preheating the oven) and refrigerated. Remove from the refrigerator 30 minutes before baking.

3 medium tomatoes

3 tablespoons mayonnaise

1 teaspoon Dijon mustard

1 tablespoon finely chopped
  fresh parsley

2 teaspoons finely chopped
  fresh chives

3 tablespoons freshly grated
  Parmesan cheese

salt and freshly ground black pepper

Garnish

1 tablespoon finely chopped
  fresh parsley

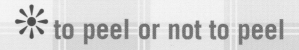

✳ to peel or not to peel

Cooks are split over whether or not to peel tomatoes. I enjoy their skin when I am eating them raw, but I prefer to peel and seed them before cooking them in sauce. The best way to peel tomatoes is to immerse them in a large pan of boiling water for 10 seconds and remove them immediately. Run cold water over the tomatoes to cool them and then peel them. To seed the tomatoes, cut them in half and carefully squeeze out the seeds and some of the juice. (You may need to ease out the seed sacs with a fingertip or a knife tip.) Or peel, seed, and puree them all at once by running them through a food processor and straining the puree.

Vine-ripened tomatoes are an essential element of the summer table. Biting into a sun-warmed, perfectly ripe tomato is a definite reward of the season. While we are used to enjoying the classic red tomato, we now have the option of eating yellow, orange, green striped, and even white ones, too. The types most widely available include:

tomatoes

Plum	*These small, pear-shaped tomatoes, also known as Roma tomatoes, are 2 to 3 inches long. They are firm-fleshed and are excellent for sauces and ratatouille. They are also good for salads and are the tomato choice for sun-drying.*
Cherry	*Available in red, orange, or yellow, these sweet little gems come in round and pear shapes. The yellow and orange varieties tend to be less acidic. When tiny, toss them whole into a salad, or halve larger ones.*
Beefsteak	*This is the king of tomatoes in both size and flavor. Beefsteaks are now also available in green and yellow, as well as the usual red.*

A Few Quick Ways to Enjoy Tomatoes:

- *Mix red and yellow, round or pear-shaped tomatoes with oil and vinegar and shredded basil. Mound the mixture on a dark-colored plate for striking contrast.*
- *Layer tomatoes with sliced fresh mozzarella. Sprinkle with olive oil and balsamic vinegar and garnish with strips of sun-dried tomato and basil.*
- *Spread tomato halves with Roasted Garlic Mayonnaise (page 186) and glaze under the broiler just before serving.*
- *Make the ultimate BLT by spreading basil-flavored mayonnaise on toasted French bread and layering it with crisp bacon, sliced tomatoes, and young butter lettuce.*
- *Halve and scoop out the pulp of cherry tomatoes. Spoon a dollop of Tapenade (page 184) into each tomato and garnish with a parsley leaf. Serve as an easy first course.*

cubanblackbeans

SERVES 6–8

Here, long-simmered black beans are flavored with a puree of onion and red sweet pepper and seasoned with rich balsamic vinegar. The flavor of the dish actually improves if the beans are refrigerated overnight and then reheated before serving. My friend Emmy Smith, who gave me this recipe, suggests serving Cuban Black Beans with Tomato-Papaya-Mint Salsa (page 193) for a sensational combination of flavors.

1. Pick over the beans, then rinse well. Place in a large bowl with water to cover generously and let soak overnight. Alternatively, use a quick-soak method: bring the beans to a boil in water to cover, boil for 2 minutes, remove from the heat, cover, and let stand for 1 hour.

2. Drain the soaked beans and put them in a large, heavy pot. Add enough water (about 2 quarts) to cover generously. Add the halved onions and green peppers, oregano, ham hock, and whole garlic cloves. Bring to a boil, reduce the heat to low, and simmer, uncovered, until the mixture is slightly thickened and the beans are tender, 1½ to 2 hours.

3. Remove all the large pieces of vegetables and the ham hock. Season the beans with salt, then drain them, reserving about ½ cup of the liquid. Pour the beans into a medium baking dish.

4. In a medium skillet over medium heat, warm the vegetable oil. Add the chopped onion and sauté until slightly softened, about 3 minutes. Add the red pepper and sauté for 3 minutes longer. Add the minced garlic and sauté for another minute.

5. Transfer the contents of the skillet to a food processor, add the reserved bean liquid, and puree until smooth. Add the puree to the black beans along with the vinegar and cayenne pepper. Stir to combine. Taste for seasoning. Cover and refrigerate overnight.

6. When ready to serve, reheat the beans in a 350°F oven for 30 minutes. Serve immediately.

Advance Preparation: This may be prepared 3 days in advance and refrigerated. Remove from the refrigerator 1 hour before reheating. Reheat in a 350°F oven for 30 minutes.

1 pound (2¼ cups) black beans

2 medium onions, halved, plus 1 large onion, finely chopped

2 medium green peppers, halved

1 tablespoon finely chopped fresh oregano, or 1 teaspoon dried oregano

1 large ham hock, about 1 pound

3 whole garlic cloves, plus 2 medium garlic cloves, minced

salt

3 tablespoons vegetable oil

1 large red sweet pepper, seeded and finely chopped

¼ cup tablespoons balsamic vinegar

pinch of cayenne pepper

with red pepper vinaigrette
chilledasparagus

SERVES 4–6

Springtime signals the arrival of asparagus in the market, to be enjoyed into the summer. Chilled asparagus is especially refreshing for a luncheon or a casual dinner. I am always experimenting with different variations on vinaigrette, and this one was created especially for these slender spears. A puree of red sweet pepper is added to the dressing to give it a distinctive color and taste. Toasted pine nuts and chopped red pepper garnish the finished dish. Serve the asparagus on a buffet table or as a first course. For a main course, offer Crispy Roasted Chicken with Spinach Pesto Cream (page 119) or Whole Poached Salmon with Pesto-Cucumber Sauce (page 103).

1. To make the vinaigrette, in a food processor, combine the garlic, shallot, and red pepper and process until minced. Add the vinegars, lemon juice, mayonnaise, basil, and salt and pepper to taste. Process until combined. With the motor running, slowly add the olive oil, processing until blended. Taste for seasoning. Set aside.
2. Bring a large sauté pan of salted water to a boil and add the asparagus. Boil until just tender, about 5 minutes. (They will continue to cook a bit longer off the heat.) With a slotted spoon or tongs, transfer to paper towels to drain.
3. Arrange the asparagus on a rectangular serving platter. Cover and refrigerate until chilled, about 2 hours.
4. To prepare the garnish, preheat the oven to 350°F. Toast the pine nuts until lightly browned, about 5 minutes.
5. When ready to serve, pour the vinaigrette evenly over the asparagus. Garnish with the red pepper and pine nuts and serve immediately.

Advance Preparation: This may be prepared 8 hours in advance through step 4 and refrigerated until ready to serve. Garnish just before serving.

Vinaigrette

2 medium garlic cloves

1 medium shallot

3 tablespoons finely chopped red sweet pepper

2 tablespoons red wine vinegar

1 tablespoon balsamic vinegar

2 teaspoons fresh lemon juice

1 tablespoon mayonnaise

1 tablespoon finely chopped fresh basil

salt and freshly ground black pepper

½ cup olive oil

2 pounds asparagus, preferably thin, tough ends trimmed and spears peeled

Garnish

2 tablespoons pine nuts

2 tablespoons finely chopped red sweet pepper or roasted red sweet pepper (page 196)

grilled**corn**on**the**cob
with ancho chile butter

Corn on the cob, grilled in the husk on the barbecue, is an earthy change of pace. If you are having an informal party, it's fun to use the peeled-back husks to hold the corn. If this is too rustic for you, detach the husks and use corn holders. Serve with your favorite barbecued ribs or Grilled Steaks, California Style (page 129) and salad or coleslaw.

1. To make the chile butter, in a small bowl, beat together the chile paste, butter, and salt to taste until thoroughly blended. Reserve.
2. Pull back the husks from the ears of the corn, being careful not to break them off. Remove all the silk inside.
3. Soak the corn in a large bowl or sink full of cold water for 30 minutes to 1 hour.
4. Prepare the barbecue for medium-heat grilling.
5. Drain the corn and pat dry. Rub with some of the butter. Replace the husks around the ears.
6. Grill the ears about 3 inches from the fire, turning to cook evenly, for 10 to 15 minutes; the timing depends on their size.
7. Remove from the grill and, using a pot holder glove, remove the husks.
8. Serve immediately with the remaining butter.

Advance Preparation: This may be prepared 4 hours ahead through step 5 (except preparing the barbecue) and kept covered at room temperature.

Ancho Chile Butter

2 tablespoons Ancho Chile Paste
    (page 195)

½ cup (1 stick) unsalted butter,
    at room temperature

salt

6 ears white or yellow corn,
    husks left on

One of the joys of summer is choosing corn, just picked and with the husks still attached, so you can enjoy its garden-fresh sweetness. Although it's difficult to go wrong this time of year, remember these tips when selecting ears:

- Look for fresh green husks and tender milky kernels that are plump and leave no space between the rows.
- Don't buy ears with gigantic kernels.
- Corn does not keep well and its delicious sugar will quickly turn to starch, so store it very cold and for only a short time. A cooler filled with ice will keep the corn at its best for a few hours.
- If at all possible, eat corn the same day it is picked.

Some corn varieties read like new ice cream flavors:

Butter and Sugar: White and yellow, very sweet corn.

Butterfruit: Crunchy yellow and sometimes white and yellow; great used raw in salads.

Early Extra Sweet: Tender yellow kernels that are especially sweet.

Early Sunglow: Among the sweetest and tenderest corn.

How Sweet It Is: White with crispy kernels.

Kandy Korn: A yellow, starchy, sweet corn.

Peaches and Cream: Sweet and juicy yellow and white kernels; good for eating raw.

Silver Queen: Sometimes called the Queen of Corn, this one boasts white, tender, crisp, sweet kernels.

Tendertreat: Yellow with creamy, rather than crunchy, kernels.

How to Cook Corn

- Drop the ears in a large pot of boiling water and cook for 2 to 4 minutes. Remove the ears with tongs and serve immediately with plenty of unsalted butter.
- You can also barbecue corn so that the kernels almost caramelize, for a deep, rich flavor.

greencorntamales

SERVES 8–12

These spectacularly good tamales should be made at the peak of the corn season. If you're lucky enough to find white corn, you will have the sweetest, most delicate tamales imaginable. A touch of fresh jalapeño chile is added to the corn mixture for a subtle bite, and the sour cream–based sauce is a refreshing accompaniment. ✳ *Since this is one of those elaborate dishes that requires lots of time and help, invite your friends who love to cook. Split up the jobs of husking and shucking the corn so that everyone is involved. Filling the tamales and folding them into neat little packages takes a bit of experience, so don't get discouraged if your first few aren't perfect. They'll still taste good.* ✳ *Serve this as a first course followed by Roasted Sea Bass with Herbs (page 100) or as a light main course with plenty of sliced ripe tomatoes on the side.*

1. With a large, sharp knife, cut off the stem from each ear of corn. Cut off any long and straggly husks. The husks should just hug the ears.
2. Cut through the corn husks about ¼ inch up from the base of the ear, cutting just through the husks but not into the corn. Remove the husks one by one. They will roll up to resemble a roll of paper. Discard the husks that are torn or too small, usually the outer and innermost leaves.
3. With a small knife, cut the corn kernels off the cob. To do this, hold the ear in a very large bowl and scrape the kernels off the cob into the bowl. Discard the cobs.
4. In a food processor, combine 4 cups of the corn kernels with a handful of the cheese and process until completely pureed. Pour into a large bowl. Repeat with the remaining corn kernels and cheese, working in batches. Add the cornmeal, chile, and salt and mix well.
5. Lay 2 husks end to end on a work surface, with the 2 wide ends overlapping by about 2 inches. Spoon about ¼ cup of the corn mixture in the center. Be careful not to overfill; the amount of filling may vary according to the size of the husks. Lift the side nearest to you and roll it in the opposite direction, encasing the filling. Fold over the two long ends to encase and secure the filling completely, pushing the filling toward the center as you do. Place seam side down on a platter.

30 ears corn, husks left on

2 pounds Monterey Jack or mild Cheddar cheese, shredded

1 cup yellow cornmeal

1 jalapeño chile, seeded and finely chopped (see note)

1 tablespoon salt

Sauce

2 cups sour cream

¾ cup Tomatillo Sauce (page 189)

6. When ready to cook, pour water to a depth of 2 inches into a 6-quart Dutch oven or other heavy pot. Lay a steaming rack on the bottom of the pot. Line the sides of the pot vertically with husks. Arrange a layer of tamales on the steaming rack, covering the rack completely. Then top with additional layers until the pot is full. Fold over the husks from the sides of the pot to cover the tamales. Flatten additional husks over the top to cover the tamales completely. Repeat the process in a second pot with the remaining tamales.

7. Place over high heat, cover, and steam until the filling is just firm enough to hold its shape, about 30 minutes.

8. While the tamales are cooking, make the sauce: Combine the sour cream and Tomatillo Sauce in the food processor and process until pureed. Taste for seasoning. If you like it very spicy, add another finely chopped jalapeño chile.

9. When the tamales are cooked, transfer them to a serving platter and serve the sauce on the side. Don't forget a large bowl for the discarded husks.

Advance Preparation: Although this is best made and cooked right before serving, the tamales may be steamed up to 3 hours ahead and kept warm in the pot. The husks will keep them warm.

Note: When working with chilies, always wear rubber gloves. Wash the cutting surface and knife immediately afterward.

It's a common misconception that chilies are used in cooking only to add hotness. In fact, their flavors add depth and complexity to a dish, and they can play a significant role in summer cooking. Different chilies have completely different properties and each will add their own distinctive character. The fire in all chilies is concentrated in the seeds and the ribs or veins, the little strips running down the inner surface of the chile. Remember always to wear rubber gloves when working with chilies and to clean the cutting surface and knife immediately afterward. Here's a quick primer on some favorite chilies:

chilies

Anaheim

Also called the New Mexico chile, the chile verde, and the mild green chile, this is the chile to use when you want a mild taste. It is also excellent for stuffing. The Anaheim is medium-light green turning to dark bright green and is 6 to 7 inches long. It must be roasted and peeled before using and is available fresh as well as whole or diced in cans.

Poblano

This popular chile has an almost triangular shape and a deep, rich flavor. About 5 inches long, it must be roasted and peeled before using. Its hotness can vary from mild to fairly hot, so taste the chile to make sure it will not overwhelm your dish. It is good added to soups, salsas, and sauces.

Jalapeño

Bright to dark green and extremely hot, the jalapeño is short and stubby, usually about 2 inches long. It is available fresh and canned and is an excellent addition to salsas, sauces, dressings, and marinades. It does not need to be roasted and peeled, but be sure to seed it.

Serrano — Sold at both its dark green and scarlet stages, this skinny little pepper has a rich and spicy character. It does not need to be roasted and peeled, but it must be seeded to avoid excessive heat. It's great with salsa, sauces, main dishes, and as a garnish for dishes that contain it.

Ancho — Wrinkled looking and mildly hot, this chile is 4 to 5 inches long, and has a triangular shape and a rich mahogany red color. It is the ripened, dried version of the poblano chile, and is available in Mexican specialty stores and in the specialty section of supermarkets. For maximum flavor, it should be toasted over high heat in a skillet until it begins to puff up. Pour boiling water over it to soften it before using.

Chipolte — The chipotle is a smoked and dried version of the jalapeño. It is moderately hot, has a distinctive smoky flavor, and is widely available canned in adobo sauce, a mixture of garlic, tomatoes, and vinegar.

Red Pepper Flakes — This is dried hot pepper that has been crushed with the seeds inside, which means that it's very hot and should be used sparingly.

Store fresh chilies in a plastic bag in the crisper for up to 1 week. They are excellent in marinades, salsas, vegetables, rice, soups, and egg dishes. Dried chilies may be kept almost indefinitely. Try toasting them in a dry pan over medium heat before using, to intensify their flavor.

lemon-herb roasted potatoes

Here, potatoes are roasted with simple seasonings to a crispy golden brown outside, while the flesh stays moist and flavorful. They'll highlight many main dishes without overpowering them. Serve with Scrambled Eggs with Three Cheeses (page 63), Sautéed Chicken with Tomato-Leek Sauce (page 114), or Grilled Veal Chops with Grilled Summer Salsa (page 133).

1. Preheat the oven to 425°F.
2. In a large bowl, stir together the olive oil, lemon juice, oregano, thyme, paprika, and salt and pepper to taste. Add the potatoes and toss to coat evenly.
3. Arrange the potatoes in a single layer on an oiled baking sheet. Bake, turning every 15 minutes, until tender and well browned, about 35 minutes. Taste for seasoning.
4. Transfer to a serving dish and serve immediately.

Advance Preparation:

This may be prepared 2 hours in advance and kept covered at room temperature. Reheat in a 350°F oven for 10 to 15 minutes.

¼ cup olive oil

2 tablespoons fresh lemon juice

1 teaspoon fresh oregano, or ½ teaspoon dried oregano

1 teaspoon fresh thyme, or ½ teaspoon dried thyme

¼ teaspoon paprika

salt and freshly ground black pepper

2½ pounds small Red Rose or White Rose potatoes, unpeeled, cut into ¾-inch-dice

grilled red potatoes

SERVES 4–6

If you can't find tiny potatoes for this recipe, use larger ones and cut them into 1½-inch pieces. When cooked in aluminum foil, the potatoes steam while the pesto and cheese form a crispy coating. As you open the foil packages, their fragrance fills the air. You will get nearly the same result if you bake them in the oven. Serve the potatoes as a side dish with simple grilled chicken or fish.

1. Bring a large pot of water to a boil over medium-high heat, add the potatoes, and boil for 10 minutes. Remove from the heat and pour into a colander. Let cool.
2. Prepare the barbecue for medium-heat grilling (or preheat the oven to 425°F).
3. Cut six 6-inch square pieces of aluminum foil.
4. Place 3 potatoes on each piece of foil. Spoon 1 teaspoon Spinach Pesto on top of each portion and then sprinkle each with ½ teaspoon Parmesan cheese. Bring up the sides of the foil and secure closed.
5. Grill the potato packages 3 inches from the flame, turning once, for 6 to 8 minutes on each side. If using the oven, place the packages on a baking sheet and bake for 25 to 35 minutes. To test for doneness, carefully open a package and pierce a potato with a knife tip.
6. Transfer the potato packages to a serving platter and open the packages just before serving.

Advance Preparation: This may be prepared 8 hours in advance through step 4 (except for preparing the barbecue or preheating the oven) and refrigerated. Remove from the refrigerator 30 minutes before grilling or baking.

1½ pounds baby red potatoes
(16 to 18), unpeeled

2 tablespoons Spinach Pesto
(page 192)

1 tablespoon freshly grated
Parmesan cheese

herbed new potatoes
with vermouth

SERVES 4

These dressed-up potatoes look particularly pretty with a strip of peel removed from around the middle. Steaming the potatoes brings out their innate sweetness. The vermouth-and-herb-flavored butter adds a gentle, yet striking, contrast. Serve with Grilled Halibut in Lemon-Mustard-Tarragon Marinade (page 101), Roasted Rosemary-Lemon Chicken (page 118), or Grilled Marinated Flank Steak (page 128).

1. Either peel the potatoes, or just peel a ring around the middle of each one for a decorative look.
2. Place on a steamer rack over boiling water, cover, and steam until tender, 15 to 20 minutes.
3. In a small saucepan over medium heat, combine all the remaining ingredients, including salt and pepper to taste, and heat until the butter melts. Taste for seasoning.
4. Transfer the potatoes to a serving bowl and pour the butter over them. Serve immediately.

Advance Preparation: These may be kept warm in the top of a double boiler over hot water for 1 hour.

1½ pounds small new potatoes
(16 to 18)

2 tablespoons unsalted butter

2 tablespoons dry vermouth

2 teaspoons finely chopped
fresh chives

1 tablespoon finely chopped
fresh mint

salt and freshly ground white pepper

desserts

poached**peaches**

in white zinfandel with raspberry sauce

SERVES 6

I created this recipe when my first crop of Babcock peaches turned out to be larger than I had expected. The Babcock peach is distinctive because of its creamy white fruit streaked with red.

1. Bring a large saucepan of water to a boil. Immerse the peaches in the water for about 20 seconds, then remove immediately. Let cool, then peel the peaches, cut in half, and remove the pits.

2. In a large nonaluminum Dutch oven or other heavy pot over medium heat, combine the wine, sugar, cinnamon sticks, and mint sprigs. Bring to a simmer, stirring to dissolve the sugar.

3. Carefully slip the peach halves into the pan. Cover and poach until tender but still firm, about 10 minutes. (The timing will depend on the ripeness and size of the peaches.) Turn the peaches at least once during poaching to ensure an even color.

4. Using a slotted spoon, transfer the peaches to a nonaluminum bowl and let cool. Let the syrup cool in the pan, remove and discard the mint leaves, and drizzle about ½ cup of the syrup over the cooled peaches.

5. To make the raspberry sauce, in a blender or food processor, puree the berries. Add the lemon juice and confectioners' sugar and process until smooth. Strain the puree through a nylon sieve placed over a bowl, using a rubber spatula to push the sauce through the sieve. Cover and refrigerate until needed.

6. To serve, arrange 2 peach halves in each individual glass bowl. Top each with a tablespoon or so of the syrup and then spoon on some of the raspberry sauce. Garnish with fresh mint leaves.

Advance Preparation: This may be prepared 8 hours in advance through step 5 and refrigerated.

Variation: The peaches can be poached whole. Increase the cooking time slightly and serve with a knife and fork, since the pit has not been removed.

Note: Babcock peaches and other white peaches cook faster than the yellow varieties.

6 medium, slightly firm Babcock or
  other white peaches
3 cups white Zinfandel
1 cup granulated sugar
2 cinnamon sticks
10 fresh mint sprigs, preferably
  pineapple mint

Sauce

1 pint fresh raspberries, or ¾ pound
  frozen unsweetened raspberries,
  thawed and drained
1 tablespoon fresh lemon juice
2 tablespoons confectioners' sugar

Garnish

fresh mint leaves, preferably
  pineapple mint

Fruit salad is often the answer to the question of what to serve on the hottest days. It is one of the few dishes appropriate for breakfast, brunch, lunch, and dinner. Mixing peak-of-the-season fruits in a large bowl and tossing them together with a little fresh lemon juice to preserve their color is the everyday way to make fruit salad. Here are a few more elaborate suggestions:

- *Using a melon baller, make melon balls from watermelon (red and yellow, if possible) and Crenshaw and orange honeydew melons and combine in a large glass bowl. Flavor with a sweet liqueur. Passion fruit liqueur is especially good, but the orange-flavored ones also work well. Decorate with fresh mint sprigs. A good creamy dressing to serve on the side is plain yogurt mixed with crème fraîche and flavored with a few drops of the same liqueur.*
- *Cut peeled Babcock peaches in half and remove the pit. Fill the hollow of each peach half with raspberries and finish with a dollop of crème fraîche and a sprig of mint.*
- *Combine peeled and diced papaya and avocado and dress with fresh lemon juice. In the Caribbean, the papaya seeds are served with the papaya and much enjoyed for their peppery taste. Add them to the mixture for an interesting accent.*

Combination fruit platters can be beautiful to look at as well as wonderful to eat. Here's just one idea, meant for a large party, to inspire you:

- *Arrange very thinly sliced triangles of red and yellow watermelon, with rind intact, along the edge of one part of the platter. Continue the border of fruit, using other thinly sliced melons such as honeydew, Crenshaw, cantaloupe, and Persian. In the center of the platter, alternate yellow and white peach slices that have been brushed with fresh lemon juice. Slice purple and yellow plums and arrange them in an informal pattern. Wedges of nectarine, papaya, and mango, also brushed with fresh lemon or lime juice, complete the sliced fruits. Place red raspberries around the peaches, strawberries around the plums, and blueberries around the mangoes and papayas. Garnish the edge of the platter with pesticide-free lemon and camellia leaves.*

 summer fruit salads and platters

summerfruitcompote

In this seasonal compote, bright fruits are gently poached together in a Johannisberg Riesling syrup. The wine has a semidry, fruity character that complements summer's harvest. You can vary the fruits you poach, but make sure that they are all about the same size. You will need to undercook them slightly, as they continue to cook while cooling. Accompany the compote with a plate of Toasted Almond Cookies with Lemon and Port (page 174) or your favorite biscotti.

1. Bring a large saucepan of water to a boil. Immerse the peaches in the water for about 20 seconds, then remove immediately with a slotted spoon. Let cool, then peel the peaches, cut in half, and remove the pits. Place in a medium bowl.

2. Immerse the plums in the same boiling water for 1 to 1½ minutes, then remove with a slotted spoon. Let cool, then peel the plums. Place in the bowl with the peaches.

3. In a large saucepan, combine the wine, sugar, and lemon slices and bring to a boil over high heat, stirring to dissolve the sugar. Reduce the heat to medium-low so the liquid is at a gentle simmer.

4. Add the peaches, plums, and apricots to the syrup, cover, and simmer, turning occasionally until the fruits are just tender. The apricots may be ready before the other fruits, so watch carefully and remember that all the fruits will continue to cook for a few minutes after they are removed from the syrup. As soon as the fruits are done, transfer them to a large glass bowl with a slotted spoon. They should be slightly resitant when cut.

5. Raise the heat to high and boil the syrup to reduce by one-half. Remove from the heat, remove and discard the lemon slices, and let the syrup cool.

6. Pour the cooled syrup over the fruit, cover, and refrigerate for 4 to 6 hours.

7. To serve, garnish the bowl with mint leaves. Serve crème fraîche or whipped cream on the side, if desired.

Advance Preparation: This may be prepared 1 day in advance through step 6 and refrigerated.

6 medium, slightly underripe peaches

6 medium, slightly underripe plums

3 cups Johannisberg Riesling

1 cup sugar

2 thick lemon slices

6 medium, slightly underripe apricots

Garnish

fresh mint leaves

crème fraîche or whipped cream (optional)

strawberry**shortcake**

SERVES 8

These shortcake biscuits melt in your mouth. A chunky sauce of pureed and sliced strawberries is spooned over the biscuits, and a cool, soothing custard enriched with whipped cream and raspberry liqueur replaces the customary whipped cream topping. Any combination of berries or fruits may be substituted for the strawberries.

1. To make the sauce, in the top pan of a medium-size double boiler, combine the egg yolks, sugar, and liqueur and beat until well blended.
2. Place over medium-low heat (the water should just be simmering) and whisk vigorously until the mixture becomes foamy and begins to thicken. Remove from the heat, add ¼ cup of the cream, and whisk until blended. Pour into a medium bowl to cool.
3. Whip the remaining 1 cup cream until stiff.
4. Fold the whipped cream into the cooled custard, cover, and refrigerate until serving.
5. To make the filling, in a food processor, puree 2 cups of the sliced strawberries. Transfer to a medium bowl. Add the remaining strawberry slices, confectioners' sugar, and framboise. Mix gently to avoid bruising the strawberry slices. Set aside.
6. To make the shortcake, preheat the oven to 425°F.
7. In a food processor, combine the flour, baking powder, salt, and sugar and process briefly to mix. Add the butter and pulse until the mixture is the consistency of bread crumbs. With the motor running, slowly pour in the cream, processing until the mixture becomes a soft dough.
8. Transfer the dough to a floured work surface. Knead with the heel of your palm until it is well blended. Roll out ½ inch thick. Cut into 3-inch squares or rounds.
9. Place at least 2 inches apart on an ungreased baking sheet. Bake until the tops are just light brown, 10 to 12 minutes. Transfer to racks to cool.

Sauce

8 egg yolks

¼ cup sugar

¼ cup framboise or kirsch

1¼ cups whipping cream

Filling

4 pints strawberries, hulled and
 thickly sliced

¼ to ½ cup confectioners' sugar,
 to taste

1 tablespoon framboise or kirsch

Shortcake

2 cups all-purpose flour

1 tablespoon baking powder

½ teaspoon salt

2 tablespoons sugar

6 tablespoons (¾ stick) chilled
 unsalted butter, cut into
 ½-inch pieces

1 cup whipping cream

recipe continues ▶

10. To assemble, split the shortcakes horizontally and place the halves, cut sides up, on a dessert plate. Place 2 tablespoons of the strawberries on top of each half, and then pour about 2 tablespoons of the sauce over each mound of strawberries. Serve immediately. Pass the remaining sauce at the table.

Advance Preparation: The shortcakes are best if baked no more than 2 hours before serving. The strawberry filling may be prepared up to 8 hours in advance and refrigerated. The sauce may be prepared up to 1 day in advance and refrigerated.

quick fruit desserts

Sliced strawberries with balsamic vinegar

Sliced figs with crème fraîche

Sliced peaches with amarettini

Blueberries and diced nectarines with a sauce of yogurt and sour cream, dusted with ground mace

Sliced melon with a garnish of diced crystallized ginger and fresh mint leaves

raspberrypoundcake

This light, moist coffee cake is an especially nice addition to a weekend brunch. If you want to serve it as a dessert, spoon some Raspberry Custard Sauce (page 161) over each slice and garnish with raspberries. Heavy bundt pans bake unevenly, so use a lightweight one for perfect results.

1. Preheat the oven to 325°F. Butter and flour a 9-inch (9-cup) lightweight bundt pan.
2. In a large bowl, using an electric mixer set on medium speed, beat together the eggs and sugar until the mixture turns a pale lemon color. Add the butter pieces and liqueur and continue to beat until fluffy. Add all but 2 tablespoons of the flour, the baking powder, and the salt and mix well.
3. In a separate bowl, toss the raspberries with the remaining 2 tablespoons flour, coating them evenly. Fold gently into the batter.
4. Pour into the prepared pan. Bake until a toothpick inserted in the center comes out clean, about 1 hour. Transfer to a rack and let the cake cool in the pan for 20 to 25 minutes.
5. Invert the cake onto the rack, then turn it upright and place on a serving plate. Let cool completely. Dust with confectioners' sugar.

Advance Preparation:

This may be prepared 8 hours in advance, covered with aluminum foil or plastic wrap, and kept at room temperature.

Note: The cup measurement is important here. It will equal about 1½ pints.

5 eggs

1⅔ cups sugar

1¼ cups (2½ sticks) unsalted butter, at room temperature and cut into pieces

2 tablespoons kirsch, framboise, or other fruit liqueur

2½ cups all-purpose flour

1 teaspoon baking powder

½ teaspoon salt

3 cups raspberries, not overripe (see note)

Garnish

confectioners' sugar

peachmelbacobbler

SERVES 6–8

This dessert was inspired by the timeless combination of peach and raspberries. A cobbler by definition is a fruit mixture with a biscuit-style dough baked on top. Partially cooking the filling prior to adding the dough helps the dough to cook evenly. You can change this recipe to include your favorite seasonal fruits of the moment, such as blackberries or boysenberries. Just make sure to add enough sugar to sweeten the fruit you are using. Place a scoop of French vanilla ice cream alongside each serving.

1. To begin making the dough, preheat the oven to 350°F. Toast the almonds until golden brown and fragrant, 5 to 7 minutes. Let cool. Transfer to a food processor and process until finely ground. Set aside in a medium bowl.

2. Raise the oven heat to 400°F. Butter and flour a 9-by-13-inch baking dish.

3. To make the filling, in a large bowl, combine the peaches, raspberries, sugar, lemon zest, and flour and mix well. Spoon into the prepared dish. The fruit should come to within ¼ inch of the top. (You need room for the dough.)

4. Place the baking dish on a baking sheet. Bake until hot and bubbly, about 20 minutes.

5. Meanwhile, return to making the dough: Add the flour, sugar, baking powder, baking soda, and salt to the ground almonds. Cut in the butter with your fingers or 2 forks until it is the size of small peas. In a small bowl, whisk together the buttermilk, vanilla and almond extracts, and egg until blended. Pour the buttermilk mixture into the center of the flour mixture and mix well with a wooden spoon. The dough will be sticky.

6. When the fruit has cooked for 20 minutes, remove it from the oven. Using an ice cream scoop, drop the dough evenly over the surface of the hot fruit. You can spread out the dough and make it as even as you like. The more uneven the dough, the more cobbled the top will look. Sprinkle the sugar and the sliced almonds evenly over the top.

7. Return the cobbler to the oven until it is golden brown and the dough is cooked through, about 20 minutes. Let cool for 30 minutes. Serve warm.

Advance Preparation: This can be prepared up to 8 hours ahead and kept at room temperature. Serve at room temperature or reheat in a 350°F oven for 10 to 15 minutes.

Dough

½ cup sliced almonds

1½ cups all-purpose flour

5 tablespoons sugar

1½ teaspoons baking powder

1 teaspoon baking soda

½ teaspoon salt

6 tablespoons (¾ stick) chilled unsalted
    butter, cut into ¼-inch pieces

¾ cup buttermilk

1 teaspoon vanilla extract

½ teaspoon almond extract

1 egg

Filling

6 large or 10 medium peaches, cut into
    1-inch pieces (about 10 cups)

3 cups raspberries

¼ cup sugar

1 teaspoon finely chopped lemon zest

2 tablespoons all-purpose flour

Topping

2 tablespoons sliced almonds

1 tablespoon sugar

latticecrustpie

SERVES 6–8

Simple one-fruit summer pies are good, but mixed-fruit pies are even better. A quartet of fruits is baked together in this pie, but each one retains its individual texture and flavor. The juices of these four fruits cook into a thick syrup that is sweet yet tangy. The lattice crust gives the pie a fresh country look. Serve with French vanilla ice cream.

1. To make the pastry, in a food processor, combine the flour and salt and process briefly to mix. Add the butter and shortening and process until the mixture is the consistency of coarse meal, 5 to 10 seconds.

2. With the motor running, gradually add the egg, lemon juice, and 3 tablespoons ice water. Process until the dough just begins to come together and will hold a shape when pressed, add more ice water if necessary. Gather into a ball, divide in half, and flatten each half into a thick disk. Wrap in waxed paper or plastic wrap and refrigerate for 2 to 4 hours.

3. To make the filling, combine all the fruits in a medium bowl. Add the sugar, nutmeg, cinnamon, flour, and lemon juice and stir until the fruit is evenly mixed with the dry ingredients and lemon juice.

4. Preheat the oven to 425°F.

5. On a floured work surface, roll out 1 dough disk into an 11-inch round about ¼ inch in thickness. Ease 1 round over a 9-inch pie dish, and then work the pastry into the dish, crimping the edges about ½ inch above the rim. Make the egg glaze by beating together the egg and water until frothy, then brush some of it on the sides and bottom of the pie crust. Spoon the fruit into the pie, heaping it in the center.

6. Roll out the remaining dough disk into an 11-inch round. Cut it into strips about 1 inch wide.

7. Brush the edge of the pie crust with some of the glaze. Place a row of the dough strips across the pie, spacing them ¾ inch apart and pinching the ends to the rim of the crust so they adhere. Arrange the remaining strips in the opposite direction on top of the pie, so the strips, when touching, are at right angles. Brush the strips with the egg glaze.

Pastry

2 cups all-purpose flour or pastry
    flour (do not use whole-wheat
    pastry flour)

½ teaspoon salt

½ cup (1 stick) unsalted butter,
    chilled and cut into small pieces

3 tablespoons vegetable shortening,
    chilled

1 egg

1 tablespoon fresh lemon juice

3 to 4 tablespoons ice water

recipe continues ▶

8. Place the pie on a baking sheet. Bake for 10 minutes. Reduce the heat to 350°F and continue to bake until browned and bubbling, 35 to 45 minutes. Check the crust once to make sure it is not browning too quickly.
9. Transfer to a rack and let cool completely before serving.

Advance Preparation: This may be prepared 8 hours in advance and kept at room temperature until serving.

✺ after-dinner coffee alfresco

It may seem to be the most unlikely picnic beverage, but even if it's sizzling and you're sitting at the beach, there's nothing like a perfect cup of coffee to finish a meal. It's easy to pack up your espresso cups and a thermos of freshly brewed espresso. Whip some cream and store it in a container deep in the ice chest. To gild the lily, bring little containers of shaved chocolate, ground cinnamon, and strips of lemon zest. Include miniature (airline-size) bottles of liqueur. And don't forget the sugar.

Filling

1½ cups cut-up rhubarb
(½-inch pieces)
2 medium peaches, peeled or
unpeeled, pitted, and sliced
½ inch thick
1 pint strawberries, hulled and sliced
½ inch thick
2 medium purple plums, pitted and
cut into ½-inch pieces
¾ cup sugar
¼ teaspoon nutmeg, preferably
freshly grated
½ teaspoon ground cinnamon
⅓ cup all-purpose flour
3 tablespoons fresh lemon juice

Egg Glaze

1 egg
1 tablespoon water

hazelnut-plumtart

SERVES 8–10

You don't have to peel the plums for this French-style tart, which is so gorgeous your guests will think you bought it at a fancy pâtisserie. The fruit slices retain their shape and add a tangy counterpoint to the sweet hazelnut filling. I like to offer a big bowl of crème fraîche on the side. French vanilla ice cream is also good.

1. To make the pastry, in a food processor, combine the flour, confectioners' sugar, and salt and process briefly to mix. Add the butter and process until the mixture is the consistency of coarse meal, 5 to 10 seconds.
2. With the motor running, add the egg yolk and then gradually the ice water. Process until the dough just begins to come together and will hold a shape when pressed.
3. Transfer the dough to a floured work surface and press into a thick disk for easy rolling. Roll out into a round at least 11½ inches in diameter and about ¼ inch thick. Drape the dough round over the rolling pin, position it over a 10-inch tart pan with a removable bottom, and ease it into the bottom and sides of the pan, pressing the pastry gently into place. If using a pan with fluted sides, roll the rolling pin over the top edge of the pan with moderate pressure to trim away the excess dough. If using a pan with straight sides, raise the edges of the pastry ¼ to ½ inch above the rim of the pan by squeezing the dough from both sides with your index fingers. Place the tart pan on a baking sheet.
4. Preheat the oven to 400°F.
5. To make the filling, in a food processor, finely grind the hazelnuts. Add the granulated sugar, butter, flour, and hazelnut liqueur. Pulse until a meal-like paste forms. Add the eggs and process for 10 seconds to incorporate. Spread the mixture in an even layer in the pastry-lined pan.
6. To make the topping, arrange the plum slices in overlapping concentric circles on the filling. Be sure to fit them tightly together. Arrange 2 concentric rows of the plum slices in the center of the tart.
7. Dot the plums with the butter and dust with the granulated sugar. Bake until the tart is browned on top, about 1 hour. Transfer to a rack and let cool completely.

Pastry

1¼ cups all-purpose flour

1 tablespoon confectioners' sugar

pinch of salt

½ cup (1 stick) unsalted butter, frozen and cut into small pieces

1 egg yolk

2 tablespoons ice water

Filling

1½ cups sliced or chopped hazelnuts

¾ cup granulated sugar

¼ cup (½ stick) unsalted butter, at room temperature

2 tablespoons all-purpose flour

¼ cup hazelnut liqueur

2 eggs

Topping

1¼ pounds purple plums, pitted and thinly sliced

2 tablespoons unsalted butter, cut into bits

2 tablespoons granulated sugar

recipe continues ▶

8. Garnish the tart with the hazelnuts and serve.

Advance Preparation: The tart may be prepared 8 hours in advance through step 6 (except for preheating the oven) and refrigerated. The finished tart may be kept up to 6 hours in the refrigerator. Remove it from the refrigerator 1 hour before serving, as it is best served at room temperature.

Garnish

2 tablespoons sliced or chopped hazelnuts

❋ cheese and fruit combinations

A fruit and cheese platter can be a stunning ending to a simple meal or elegant buffet. I use a wicker cheese tray or other shallow basket and accent the cheeses with edible flowers from the garden. Here is the one place I think flowers belong with food, nasturtiums or roses especially. A few wonderful fruit and cheese combinations follow.

Nectarines with Explorateur or Brillat-Savarin

Apricots with mascarpone

Pears with Gorgonzola

Figs with St. Andre

Peaches with fromage blanc

Red and green seedless grapes with fresh goat cheese

Granny Smith apples with aged Monterey Jack

Melon slices with Brie

A basket of mixed nuts in their shells with
any combination of cheese and fruit

chocolatepecantorte

SERVES 6

This is the cake of choice among my confirmed chocoholic friends. It contains no fruit that might interfere with the intensity of the chocolate experience. This European-style torte, which is a covered with a chocolate glaze and decorated with chocolate-dipped pecans, is like a cooled chocolate pecan soufflé. The chilled coffee custard sauce provides a refreshing counterpoint. Just before serving, spoon a pool of sauce on a dessert plate and place a slice of cake in the center.

1. To make the crème anglaise, in a small saucepan, combine the half-and-half and vanilla bean. (If using vanilla extract, it will be added later.) Bring to a simmer over medium-high heat, remove from the heat, and cover the pan. Let stand for 20 minutes.

2. Place the egg yolks in the top pan of a double boiler over simmering water in the lower pan. Add the sugar and whisk until thick and lemon colored. Remove the vanilla bean from the half-and-half and discard. Slowly pour the hot half-and-half into the egg yolk mixture, whisking constantly. Add the espresso (and the vanilla extract, if using) and continue whisking until the mixture reaches a custardlike consistency. It should coat the back of a wooden spoon. Do not allow to boil, or the custard will curdle. Immediately remove the sauce from the heat and pour it through a fine-mesh sieve into a bowl. Place the bowl over a bowl filled with ice water and stir until the sauce is cool. Cover and refrigerate until needed.

3. To make the glaze, slowly melt the chocolate and butter in the top pan of the double boiler over simmering water, stirring until smooth. Stir in the vegetable oil and corn syrup. Remove from the heat and let cool. It should be room temperature to glaze the cake.

4. To prepare the pecans for decorating, preheat the oven to 350°F. Toast until lightly browned, about 10 minutes. Let cool, then dip half of each pecan into the glaze and place on a baking sheet lined with waxed paper. Refrigerate until set. Pour the remaining glaze into a bowl. (Keep the glaze at room temperature; do not let it harden. If it does harden, gently soften it over hot water in the double boiler until it is tepid.)

Crème Anglaise

1¼ cups half-and-half

½ vanilla bean, split lengthwise, or
     1 teaspoon vanilla extract

3 egg yolks

¼ cup sugar

2 tablespoons brewed espresso

Glaze and Decoration

6 ounces semisweet chocolate

½ cup (1 stick) unsalted butter

½ teaspoon vegetable oil

1 tablespoon light corn syrup

20 large pecan halves

recipe continues ▶

5. To make the torte, cut out a round of waxed paper to fit the bottom of an 8-inch round cake pan. Place the paper in the bottom of the pan and butter the pan sides and the paper generously.

6. Combine the chocolate and butter in the top pan of the double boiler over simmering water and melt slowly, stirring occasionally. Remove from the heat and let cool.

7. Preheat the oven to 375°F.

8. In a bowl, using an electric mixer, beat the eggs until frothy. Gradually add the sugar and beat until the mixture is a pale lemon color, about 5 minutes.

9. Fold the cooled chocolate mixture into the egg mixture and blend well. Stir in the flour and the ground pecans until well combined.

10. Pour the mixture into the prepared cake pan. Bake until the top is firm to the touch and the inside is slightly soft but not runny, 25 to 30 minutes. A tester should come out of the torte slightly wet. Transfer to a rack and let cool completely.

11. Unmold the torte onto a cake rack placed on a baking sheet lined with waxed paper. Pour the reserved glaze over the cooled torte, tilting it so that the glaze runs down the sides. If there are unglazed areas, use a long spatula to touch up the sides. When the glaze is set, carefully place the glazed pecans in a border around the edge of the torte.

12. Slide a spatula under the torte and lift it onto a cake platter lined with a doily. Serve with crème anglaise.

Advance Preparation: The finished torte may be kept up to 1 day either at room temperature or refrigerated. Remove from the refrigerator 1 hour before serving. The crème anglaise may be made up to 1 day in advance and refrigerated until serving.

Torte

6 squares (6 ounces) semisweet chocolate

¾ cup (1½ sticks) unsalted butter

4 eggs

¾ cup sugar

3 tablespoons all-purpose flour

3 tablespoons ground pecans

frozenpralinemousse

SERVES 6

I love this dessert. It's like making ice cream without an ice cream maker. Using sugar syrup rather than granulated sugar gives the mousse its creamy consistency. It is easy to make and can be kept frozen for up to 2 weeks, so it's perfect to have on hand in your freezer for last-minute entertaining. Just before serving, heat Bittersweet Hot Fudge Sauce (page 177) to pour on top. Of course, the hot fudge sauce is optional, but why not go all the way?

1. Brush an 8-by-4-by-2-inch loaf pan or any 3- or 4-cup mold with vegetable oil. Completely line the mold with plastic wrap, leaving enough overhang to fold over the top later and carefully tucking it into all the corners.
2. In a small saucepan over low heat, dissolve the sugar in the water and warm until clear. Remove from the heat.
3. In a medium bowl, combine the egg yolks and vanilla. Using an electric mixer set at low speed, slowly add the sugar syrup, beating until blended. Continue beating until the mixture is thick and a pale lemon color.
4. In a separate bowl, beat the cream until stiff.
5. Fold the egg yolk mixture into the whipped cream until the color is uniform. Fold in the praline, making sure it is evenly distributed.
6. Pour into the prepared mold and cover with the plastic wrap. Freeze for at least 6 hours.
7. To serve, invert the mousse onto a flat plate and lift off the pan. Remove the plastic wrap, and cut the mousse into 6 slices. Place the slices on individual dessert plates and decorate with additional whipped cream and praline. Serve with fudge sauce, if desired.

Advance Preparation: The mousse may be prepared up to 2 weeks in advance and frozen. Remove it from the freezer 15 minutes before slicing.

¼ cup sugar

2 tablespoons water

6 egg yolks

1 teaspoon vanilla extract

1 cup whipping cream

¾ cup Pecan Praline (page 180)

Garnish

½ cup whipped cream

½ cup Pecan Praline (page 180)

1 cup Bittersweet Hot Fudge Sauce
   (page 177; optional), heated

toasted almondcookies

MAKES
ABOUT 40
COOKIES

These light Italian-inspired cookies are best eaten as soon as you take them out of the oven, while they are still very crispy. Almonds, lemon, and port are a sublime combination. The lemon tempers the sweet port, while the almonds provide the essential taste. Pour small glasses of port for dipping the cookies.

1. Preheat the oven to 350°F. Toast the almonds until lightly colored, about 3 minutes. Let cool.
2. In a medium bowl, using an electric mixer or wooden spoon, beat together the butter and granulated sugar until creamy and fluffy.
3. Add the egg yolks, port, vanilla, and 1 teaspoon of the lemon zest and stir to combine. Slowly add the flour, stirring until completely absorbed.
4. Drop the dough by teaspoonfuls 1 inch apart on 2 ungreased baking sheets. Divide the remaining 1 teaspoon lemon zest among the cookies, topping each one with a pinch.
5. Bake until golden brown, 12 to 15 minutes. Transfer the cookies to racks to cool completely.
6. Sprinkle the cooled cookies with confectioners' sugar.

Advance Preparation: These are best made and eaten the same day. Leftover cookies can be stored in an airtight container.

1 cup finely chopped almonds

½ cup (1 stick) unsalted butter, at room temperature

½ cup granulated sugar

2 egg yolks

¼ cup tawny or other sweet port

1 teaspoon vanilla extract

2 teaspoons finely chopped lemon zest

1 cup all-purpose flour

Garnish

confectioners' sugar

crushedstrawberryicecream

This dessert has a double taste of strawberries, both crushed and sliced. The new frozen-canister-type ice cream makers that require little churning and only 20 minutes of freezing time may have taken the old-fashioned charm out of making ice cream, but they have certainly made it easier, which is nice on a hot summer day. If your ice cream maker holds less than 2 quarts, divide this recipe in half. Serve with Toasted Almond Cookies with Lemon and Port (page 174).

2½ pints strawberries, hulled and
    halved lengthwise

¼ cup sugar

2 cups whipping cream

1 cup milk

4 eggs

¾ cup sugar

2 teaspoons vanilla extract

1. Finely chop 1 cup of the halved strawberries and set aside. Sprinkle the sugar over the remaining strawberries in a medium bowl. Let stand for 30 minutes and then process the strawberries in a food processor until completely smooth. If you prefer no seeds, pour through a fine-mesh sieve. Set aside.

2. In a medium saucepan over medium-high heat, combine the cream and milk and heat until scalded. Remove from the heat.

3. In a bowl, using an electric mixer, beat the eggs until frothy. Slowly add the sugar and vanilla and beat until thick and a pale lemon color.

4. Gradually whisk 1 cup of the hot cream mixture into the egg mixture. Then gradually pour the egg-cream mixture into the saucepan while whisking constantly. Cook slowly over medium-low heat, stirring constantly, until the mixture thinly coats the back of a wooden spoon, 5 to 10 minutes. Do not overcook or the mixture will curdle. Remove from the heat, pour through the fine-mesh sieve into a medium bowl, and let cool.

5. Add the pureed strawberries to the cooled custard and mix well.

6. Pour the custard into an ice cream maker and freeze according to the manufacturer's instructions just until the ice cream begins to thicken. With the machine running, add the finely chopped strawberries. At this point the ice cream will be firm but not hard. You can either spoon it into a container and place in the freezer to harden or serve it immediately.

Advance Preparation: This may be prepared 8 hours in advance through step 5 and kept in the refrigerator.

bittersweet hot fudge sauce

MAKES 1 1/2
CUPS

I prefer a bittersweet chocolate for this recipe. The blend of butter, cream, and chocolate makes the hot sauce harden just slightly when it hits the cold ice cream. This delectable sauce is perfection with Frozen Praline Mousse (page 173) or plain ice cream.

1. In the top pan of a double boiler placed over simmering water, combine the chocolate and butter and melt slowly. When melted, whisk in the cream.
2. Pour over ice cream and serve immediately.

Advance Preparation: This may be prepared 4 hours in advance and kept barely warm in the top of the double boiler over barely simmering water. It also can be prepared up to 1 week in advance and refrigerated. Reheat slowly in the double boiler.

8 squares (8 ounces) bittersweet
chocolate, coarsely chopped
1/2 cup (1 stick) unsalted butter, cut
into small pieces
1/4 cup whipping cream

strawberry sauce

MAKES 1 CUP

Using a nylon sieve ensures that the strawberries won't pick up a metallic taste. Serve this over Crushed Strawberry Ice Cream (previous page) or Frozen Peaches and Cream (page 178).

1. In a food processor or blender, process the berries until pureed. Add the lemon juice and sugar and process until blended.
2. Strain the puree through a nylon sieve placed over a bowl, using a rubber spatula to push the sauce through the sieve.
3. Use immediately, or cover and refrigerate until needed.

Advance Preparation: This may be made 5 days in advance and refrigerated. Remove from the refrigerator 30 minutes before serving.

1 pint strawberries, hulled
1 tablespoon fresh lemon juice
2 tablespoons confectioners' sugar

frozenpeachesandcream

MAKES 2
QUARTS

The crunchy sweetness of praline and a rich peachiness are the hallmarks of this summer ice cream. Make sure to buy medium-size peaches. They are more flavorful and tend to be less watery than the large ones. While the ice cream is great on its own, adding fresh raspberries and raspberry sauce turns it into an incomparable fruit sundae.

3 pounds ripe peaches

1 cup milk

2 cups whipping cream

5 egg yolks

1 cup sugar

2 teaspoons vanilla extract

1 cup Pecan Praline (page 180)

1. Bring a large saucepan of water to a boil. Immerse the peaches in water for 20 seconds, then remove immediately. Let cool, then peel the peaches, cut in half, and remove the pits. Coarsely chop 1 pound of the peaches in a food processor and reserve. Process the remaining peaches until pureed and set aside.

2. In a medium saucepan over medium-high heat, combine the milk and the cream and heat until scalded. Remove from the heat.

3. In a medium bowl, using an electric mixer, beat the eggs until frothy. Slowly add the sugar and vanilla, beating until thick and a pale lemon color.

4. Gradually whisk 1 cup of the hot cream mixture into the egg mixture. Then gradually pour the egg-cream mixture into the saucepan while whisking constantly. Cook slowly over medium-low heat, stirring constantly, until the mixture thinly coats the back of a wooden spoon, 5 to 10 minutes. Do not overcook or the mixture will curdle. Remove from the heat, pour through a fine-mesh sieve into a medium bowl, and let cool.

5. Add the pureed peaches to the cooled custard and mix well.

6. Pour the custard into an ice cream maker and freeze according to manufacturer's instructions just until the ice cream begins to thicken. With the machine running, add the coarsely chopped peaches and the praline. At this point, the ice cream will be firm but not frozen. You can either spoon it into a container and place in the freezer to harden or serve it immediately.

Advance Preparation: This may be prepared 8 hours in advance through step 5 and kept in the refrigerator.

Note: This recipe may be halved to make 1 quart. Use 3 egg yolks.

pecanpraline

Toasting brings out the full flavor of the pecans before they are coated with a golden brown caramel. When hardened, the praline is chopped into a coarse powder. Sprinkle this delicious confection on ice cream or use it in Frozen Praline Mousse (page 173) or Frozen Peaches and Cream (page 178).

1 cup pecan pieces

⅔ cup sugar

3 tablespoons water

1. Preheat the oven to 350°F. Toast the pecans until they take on color and are fragrant, 5 to 7 minutes. Let cool, then chop coarsely in a food processor. Set aside.

2. Generously oil a baking sheet.

3. In a small, heavy saucepan, combine the sugar and water. Do not use a dark-colored pan, as you will not be able to see the color of the caramel. Dissolve the sugar in the water over low heat. Raise the heat to high and continually swirl the pan over the flame. The mixture will be bubbly. If sugar crystals form on the sides of the pan, cover the pan for 1 minute and they will dissolve. Boil until the mixture turns golden brown. It should take 6 to 8 minutes. Watch carefully, as caramel can burn easily.

4. Remove from the heat and immediately add the pecans. Mix together well, coating the nuts with the caramel.

5. Pour onto the greased baking sheet, spreading evenly, and let cool.

6. When cooled, break up the praline and place in the food processor. Pulse to chop coarsely.

7. Place in an airtight container and freeze.

Advance Preparation: This may be prepared in up to 2 months in advance and kept in the freezer.

sauces and basics

summer**vinaigrette**

This vinaigrette is chock-full of fresh herbs that will liven up any type of salad greens or fresh vegetable, cold seafood, chicken, or pasta salads.

1. In a medium bowl, combine the shallot, garlic, parsley, chives, basil, mustard, lemon juice, and vinegar and whisk until well blended. (Or place in a food processor and process until well blended.)
2. Slowly pour in the olive oil, whisking constantly (or processing) until blended. Add the salt and pepper and taste for seasoning.

Advance Preparation: This may be prepared 1 week in advance and refrigerated. Bring to room temperature and whisk before using.

1 medium shallot, finely chopped

1 medium garlic clove, minced

1 tablespoon finely chopped
    fresh parsley

1 tablespoon finely chopped
    fresh chives

1 teaspoon finely chopped fresh basil

1 teaspoon Dijon mustard

1 tablespoon fresh lemon juice

3 tablespoons red wine vinegar

¾ cup olive oil

salt and freshly ground black pepper

buttermilk dressing
with garden herbs

MAKES 2
CUPS

An all-American classic, this garden-fresh dressing is delicious with raw vegetables, lettuces, or tomatoes. If you can't find burnet, a cucumber-flavored herb, add extra parsley.

1. Combine all the ingredients in a medium bowl, including salt and pepper to taste, and whisk until blended. Taste for seasoning.

Advance Preparation: This may be prepared 5 days in advance and refrigerated.

1 cup mayonnaise

1 cup buttermilk

1 medium garlic clove, minced

1 teaspoon Dijon mustard

2 teaspoons finely chopped
    fresh burnet

2 tablespoons finely chopped
    fresh chives

1 tablespoon finely chopped fresh dill

1 tablespoon finely chopped
    fresh parsley

salt and freshly ground white pepper

tapenade

MAKES 1½ CUPS

Tapenade is to Provence what pesto is to Liguria. This strong-flavored olive paste is excellent as a dipping sauce for raw vegetables. It's also delicious spread on a baguette slice or a cracker, or it can be used to season a sauce or to flavor chicken or fish.

1. Place the olives on a wooden board. With the back of a heavy cleaver, smash them, separating the pit from the olive. Discard the pits.
2. Combine all the ingredients except the olive oil in a blender or food processor. Process until pureed. If necessary, stop the motion and use a rubber spatula to scrape down the sides of the container.
3. With the motor running, slowly add the olive oil, processing until completely absorbed. Taste for seasoning.
4. Refrigerate in an airtight container until needed.

Advance Preparation: This may be prepared 1 week in advance and refrigerated.

Variation: Add 1 can (6½ ounces) tuna, drained, in step 2.

20 oil-cured black olives

2 medium garlic cloves, minced

2 tablespoons capers, well drained

4 anchovy fillets, well drained

2 teaspoons Dijon mustard

2 tablespoons fresh lemon juice

2 tablespoons finely chopped basil

¼ cup finely chopped fresh
   Italian parsley

¼ teaspoon cayenne pepper

½ cup olive oil

roasted garlic mayonnaise

MAKES 1½ CUPS

Roasting garlic gives it a subtle, sweet, nutty taste. This variation on the classic aioli is good on salads, cold chicken, smoked fish, or cold seafood. It can also be used as a dipping sauce for vegetables.

2 medium heads garlic, tops cut off

1½ cups mayonnaise

1 tablespoon fresh lemon juice

salt and freshly ground white pepper

1. Preheat the oven to 425°F.

2. Place the garlic heads on a piece of aluminum foil, bring up the sides, and secure closed. Place on a baking sheet and bake for 45 minutes to 1 hour, or until soft. Remove from the oven and let cool.

3. When cool, squeeze the soft garlic pulp from the papery sheaths by pushing hard on the garlic head into a small bowl. You should have about 2 heaping tablespoons.

4. Add the mayonnaise, lemon juice, and salt and pepper to taste and whisk to combine. Taste for seasoning.

5. Refrigerate in an airtight container until needed.

Advance Preparation: This may be made 3 days in advance and refrigerated.

☀ flavored mayonnaises

An interesting mayonnaise can be used to spice up simple dishes. The following ingredients can be mixed into a basic mayonnaise to turn it into a real asset. Make sure that the additions are finely chopped or minced to impart the fullest flavor.

Anchovies

Ancho Chile Paste (page 195)

Basil and shallots

Fresh lemon juice and chives

Roasted sweet pepper puree

Mango chutney and curry powder

Watercress, dill, and spinach with fresh lemon juice

Tapenade (page 184)

tomatobasilsauce

This uncooked sauce is actually a mild version of a Mexican tomato salsa. Basil replaces the usual hot chilies, while red pepper flakes add just a touch of heat. Serve the sauce on hot pasta, or add a little vinaigrette to it and toss it with cooled pasta and vegetables for a garden pasta salad. It also makes an appetizing garnish for simple vegetable soups.

1. Combine all the ingredients in a medium bowl, including salt and pepper to taste, and mix well. Taste for seasoning.
2. Refrigerate in an airtight container until needed.

Advance Preparation: This sauce may be prepared 1 day in advance and refrigerated.

4 medium tomatoes, peeled, seeded, and coarsely chopped

1 medium red onion, finely chopped

2 garlic cloves, minced

6 tablespoons finely chopped fresh basil

3 tablespoons finely chopped fresh Italian parsley

2 tablespoons olive oil

¼ teaspoon red pepper flakes (optional)

salt and freshly ground black pepper

freshtomatosauce

Make this tomato sauce at the height of the tomato season. Double or triple it and keep some in your freezer for fall, after the ripe tomatoes are gone. It is lighter than a marinara sauce and can be used in place of canned crushed tomatoes in soups, sauces, or pasta.

1. In a large nonaluminum pot over medium heat, warm the olive oil. Add the onion, carrot, and celery and cook, stirring frequently to avoid buring, until softened, 5 to 7 minutes.

2. Add the tomatoes, garlic, parsley, bay leaf, oregano, and basil, cover partially, and reduce the heat to medium-low. Simmer, stirring occasionally, until thickened, about 1½ hours. Remove and discard the bay leaf.

3. Transfer to a blender or food processor and puree until smooth. Pass the sauce through a sieve or a food mill. Pour back into the saucepan, bring to a boil, and boil until reduced to about 5 cups.

4. Season taste with salt and pepper. Serve hot.

Advance Preparation: This may be made 5 days in advance and refrigerated. It also may be frozen in small containers for up to 2 months.

3 tablespoons olive oil

1 medium onion, finely chopped

1 medium carrot, peeled and finely chopped

1 celery stalk, finely chopped

4 pounds ripe tomatoes, coarsely chopped

2 large garlic cloves, minced

3 tablespoons finely chopped fresh parsley

½ bay leaf

1 tablespoon finely chopped fresh oregano

2 tablespoons finely chopped fresh basil

salt and freshly ground black pepper

tomatillo sauce

MAKES
ABOUT 2 ½
CUPS

Tomatillos are the foundation of this light, spicy green sauce. If fresh tomatillos are unavailable, you can substitute drained, canned tomatillos with a pinch of sugar. You will not, however, need to cook them. Use the sauce to flavor a vinaigrette, mix it with sour cream as a sauce, or serve it as a salsa on grilled meat or fish. It's also great on eggs and fresh corn tortillas.

1. In a large skillet over medium heat, bring the chicken stock to a simmer. Add the onion, cover, and simmer until softened, about 5 minutes.
2. Add the tomatillos, re-cover, and cook until slightly thickened, about 5 minutes.
3. Pour the contents of the skillet into a blender or food processor and process until coarsely chopped. Stir in the chilies, garlic, cilantro, cumin, lemon juice, and salt to taste. Taste for seasoning. Pour into a storage container and let cool.
4. Cover and refrigerate until needed.

Advance Preparation: This may be made 5 days ahead and refrigerated in an airtight container.

Note: When working with chilies, always wear rubber gloves. Wash the cutting surface and knife immediately afterward.

¾ cup chicken stock

1 small onion, coarsely chopped

1 pound tomatillos, husks removed
    and quartered

1 or 2 jalapeño chilies, seeded and
    finely chopped (see note)

2 medium garlic cloves, minced

3 tablespoons finely chopped
    fresh cilantro

¼ teaspoon ground cumin

1 tablespoon fresh lemon juice

salt

red**pepper–tomato**sauce

MAKES 3–4
CUPS

This sauce is especially easy because there is no need to peel the tomatoes or roast the peppers. It is excellent on pasta with the addition of poached chicken or shellfish. Or serve it on steamed vegetables with a sprinkle of grated Parmesan cheese.

1. In a large nonaluminum saucepan over medium heat, warm the olive oil. Add the onion and sauté until softened, 3 to 4 minutes.

2. Add the red peppers, tomatoes, and basil, reduce the heat to medium-low, cover partially, and cook until softened, about 20 minutes. Remove from the heat.

3. Pour the contents of the pan into a food processor or blender and puree until smooth. It will take about 1 minute.

4. Season with salt and pepper. Reheat gently before serving.

Advance Preparation: This may be prepared 3 days in advance and refrigerated. It may also be frozen for up to a month. Reheat gently.

3 tablespoons olive oil

1 medium onion, finely chopped

4 large red sweet peppers, seeded
        and thinly sliced

2 large tomatoes, finely chopped

1 medium bunch fresh basil,
        coarsely chopped

salt and freshly ground black pepper

tomato-cucumber salsa

Full of crunchy cucumber, this chunky salsa is good on grilled seafood, with Chilled Avocado Soup with Tomato-Cucumber Salsa (page 51), or as a dip for tortilla chips.

1. Combine all of the ingredients in a medium bowl, including salt to taste, and mix well. Taste for seasoning. Cover and refrigerate until needed.

Advance Preparation: This may be prepared 3 days in advance and refrigerated. Remove from the refrigerator 30 minutes before serving.

Variation: Canned jalapeño chilies may be used if fresh are not available. If using the canned chilies, omit the lemon juice.

Note: When working with chilies, always wear rubber gloves. Wash the cutting surface and knife immediately afterward.

2 large tomatoes (about 1 pound), peeled, seeded, and finely chopped

½ cup peeled, seeded, and finely chopped English cucumber

1 medium jalapeño chile, seeded and finely chopped (see note)

1 tablespoon finely chopped fresh cilantro

1 tablespoon fresh lemon juice

1 medium garlic clove, minced

salt

spinach**pesto**

MAKES 1–1½
CUPS

Spinach combined with basil yields a milder version of the traditional basil pesto. It is sometimes used without the cheese, as in the Pesto-Cucumber Sauce that accompanies Whole Poached Salmon (page 103). I prefer to add the cheese right before serving, so that I can use the sauce either way. Spinach Pesto is excellent as a flavor enhancer for soups, dressings, and sauces and as a glaze for tomatoes.

1. In a food processor, process the garlic cloves until pureed.
2. Add the basil, spinach, and parsley and process until finely chopped. Add the pine nuts and finely chop.
3. With the motor running, slowly pour in the olive oil in a fine stream and process until the oil is absorbed. Season with pepper.
4. If using Parmesan, add it just before serving and process until well blended. Taste for seasoning.
5. Refrigerate in a tightly covered container until needed.

Advance Preparation: This may be prepared 1 week in advance through step 3 and refrigerated. Add the cheese just before serving.

2 medium garlic cloves

1¼ cups fresh basil leaves (about 1 medium bunch)

1 cup spinach leaves

¼ cup fresh parsley leaves

3 tablespoons pine nuts

½ cup olive oil

freshly ground black pepper

½ cup freshly grated Parmesan cheese (optional)

tomato-papaya-mint salsa

MAKES
ABOUT 2
CUPS

Papaya and tomato may seem like an unlikely combination, but that's not so. Tropical and refreshing, this salsa goes well with grilled seafood, chicken, or black beans.

1. Combine all of the ingredients in a medium bowl, including salt to taste, and stir to combine. Cover and refrigerate until needed.

Advance Preparation: This may be prepared in the morning and refrigerated.

Note: When working with chilies, always wear rubber gloves. Wash the cutting surface and knife immediately afterward.

2 large tomatoes (about 1 pound),
   peeled, seeded, and diced

1 cup peeled, seeded, and diced
   ripe papaya

1 jalapeño chile, seeded and finely
   chopped (see note)

1 shallot, finely chopped

3 tablespoons finely chopped
   fresh mint

2 tablespoons fresh lime juice

salt

apricot-plumsauce

MAKES 4
CUPS

I often double this recipe and bring it to friends as a house gift. The sauce is particularly good with pork, chicken, quail, and game hens. Dilute it with wine or nectar to use it as a marinade.

1. In a food processor, combine the onion, garlic, ginger, limes, apricots, and plums and process until pureed.

2. In a medium nonaluminum Dutch oven or other heavy pot, combine the pureed ingredients and all of the remaining ingredients except the cilantro. Bring to a boil over medium-high heat, reduce the heat to medium-low, and simmer until slightly thickened, about 45 minutes. Stir frequently to prevent burning.

3. Remove from the heat and let cool. Stir in the cilantro and taste for seasoning. Pour the sauce into a large glass container, cover, and refrigerate.

Advance Preparation: This may be prepared 2 months in advance and refrigerated.

1 large onion, coarsely chopped

4 garlic cloves, minced

¼ cup peeled and coarsely chopped fresh ginger

2 limes, thinly sliced

1 pound apricots, pitted and coarsely chopped

1 pound plums, pitted and coarsely chopped

1 cup cider vinegar

½ cup tawny port

2 cups firmly packed dark brown sugar

1 teaspoon ground cinnamon

1 teaspoon ground allspice

½ teaspoon cayenne pepper or red pepper flakes

1 teaspoon salt

¼ cup finely chopped fresh cilantro

anchochilepaste

MAKES ¼
CUP

This rustic paste has an unusual, very rich taste. The garlic and ancho chile are first "toasted," a Mexican technique that intensifies flavors. The chile is then softened and pureed into a thick paste. It is a wonderful condiment to have on hand. Try adding a spoonful to sour cream, mayonnaise, or butter. It also makes a spicy coating for meat to be grilled or roasted.

1. In a small skillet over medium-high heat, toast the garlic cloves, turning them as they begin to brown. When light brown in color, remove from the heat. Let cool slightly, then peel and set aside.

2. In the same skillet over medium heat, warm the chilies until they begin to expand and the flesh becomes soft. The chilies should smell rich, but not be charred. Remove from the heat. Let cool.

3. Wearing rubber gloves, slit the chilies open and remove the seeds and any veins. Place the chilies in a small bowl, pour boiling water over them to cover, and let soften for 15 minutes. Remove from the water and drain well.

4. In a food processor, combine the chilies and garlic and process until pureed. Add the olive oil and salt and process until well combined. Taste for seasoning. Store in an airtight container in the refrigerator until needed.

Advance Preparation: This may be prepared 1 month in advance and refrigerated.

2 large garlic cloves, unpeeled

6 large ancho chilies
    (about 3 ounces)

boiling water, to cover

3 tablespoons olive oil

salt

roasted sweet peppers or chilies

Here's a technique recipe for perfectly roasted and peeled peppers or chilies. They are broiled or grilled on the barbecue to char them, then left in a paper bag to steam, which makes peeling them easier. Although you may think this is tedious the first time you try it, you'll find it actually takes little time, and the delicious results are well worth the effort. Keep the peppers covered with oil if you are preparing them in advance. They can be added to many recipes and are also excellent served alone, dressed with a light vinaigrette. If serving sweet peppers alone, place them in a serving dish and pour the dressing over them. Sprinkle with chopped fresh basil and decorate with small Niçoise olives. Serve at room temperature or slightly chilled.

1. Preheat the broiler, or prepare a barbecue for medium-high-heat grilling.
2. Place the peppers or chilies on a broiler pan or on the grill about 6 inches from the heat. Broil or grill until blackened on all sides. Use tongs to turn the peppers or chilies to blacken evenly.
3. Transfer the peppers or chilies to a paper bag, close tightly, and let stand for 10 minutes.
4. Remove the peppers or chilies from the bag, drain, and peel off the skins. Make a slit in each pepper or chile and open it up. Remove the core, stem, seeds, and ribs. When working with chilies, always wear rubber gloves and wash the cutting surface and knife immediately afterward.
5. With a sharp knife or pizza wheel, cut the peppers or chilies as directed in individual recipes.

Advance Preparation: This may be prepared 5 days in advance and refrigerated. Remove from the refrigerator 30 minutes before using.

Red, yellow, green, or purple sweet peppers or Anaheim or poblano chilies

index

tableofequivalents

The exact equivalents in the following tables have been rounded for convenience.

Liquid/Dry Measures

U.S	METRIC
¼ teaspoon	1.25 milliliters
½ teaspoon	2.5 milliliters
1 teaspoon	5 milliliters
1 tablespoon (3 teaspoons)	15 milliliters
1 fluid ounce (2 tablespoons)	30 milliliters
¼ cup	60 milliliters
⅓ cup	80 milliliters
½ cup	120 milliliters
1 cup	240 milliliters
1 pint (2 cups)	480 milliliters
1 quart (4 cups, 32 ounces)	960 milliliters
1 gallon (4 quarts)	3.84 liters
1 ounce (by weight)	28 grams
1 pound	454 grams
2.2 pounds	1 kilogram

Oven Temperature

FAHRENHEIT	CELSIUS	GAS
250	120	½
275	140	1
300	150	2
325	160	3
350	180	4
375	190	5
400	200	6
425	220	7
450	230	8
475	240	9
500	260	10

Length

U.S.	METRIC
⅛ inch	3 millimeters
¼ inch	6 millimeters
½ inch	12 millimeters
1 inch	2.5 centimeters